REFLECTIONS OF A
SCOTTISH CHURCHMAN

THE CATHEDRAL, GLASGOW

REFLECTIONS OF A SCOTTISH CHURCHMAN

by

NEVILE DAVIDSON

Minister of Glasgow
Chaplain to the Queen in Scotland

HODDER AND STOUGHTON

To the people of Glasgow
and especially to the congregation
of the Cathedral Church of St. Mungo:
In gratitude and affection.

© 1965 by Hodder and Stoughton Ltd.

First printed 1965

Printed in Great Britain for Hodder and Stoughton Ltd.,
St. Paul's House, Warwick Lane, London, E.C.4 by
T. and A. Constable Ltd., Hopetoun Street, Edinburgh.

CONTENTS

INTRODUCTION

The essays, addresses and sermons contained in this volume cover a fairly wide range of subjects. Many of them attempt, although all too briefly, to touch upon rather large themes. But it has for long been assumed in Scotland that the ordinary intelligent layman is capable of turning his mind to the grandest and profoundest questions. Men (and women) of former generations, brought up on the Shorter Catechism and the Westminster Confession of Faith, were accustomed to theological discourses of formidable calibre. This tradition of 'plain living and high thinking' may in more recent times have been partially lost. But I believe there are signs that there is a revival of interest, often in most unexpected quarters, in some of the supreme issues affecting human life, duty, and destiny. I even dare to believe that many people in our time would welcome more theological preaching from our pulpits—especially if more opportunities were also afforded for subsequent discussion and informal exchange of views.

The ideas, propounded in rather desultory form, in this book are the fruit of some thirty years in the ordained ministry, spent in three large Scottish cities. They are the fruit of reflection on the great themes of Christian doctrine coloured, confirmed and illustrated by pastoral experience; because the clergyman, the parish minister, is never concerned only with abstract ideas, but always with ideas, convictions, beliefs as they affect men and women, in the myriad ordinary situations of life.

Inevitably, in the preparation of such a book as this, one is almost compelled to face the question: What is the place and calling of the minister of religion in the modern world? Or indeed has he any proper place?

The indispensability of the minister of religion has until now been seldom questioned by the great majority of people in Britain, any more than in other Western lands. In a country like our own, which has professed itself at least nominally Christian for some fifteen hundred years, the clergyman has been an accepted figure in society, regarded by many with tolerance, by many with respect, and by some with gratitude and affection. It has been assumed that his office is at least as necessary to the well-being of the community as that, for example, of the doctor, the schoolmaster, or the lawyer, that it is necessary to have a person trained in Divinity to lead others in worship on Sundays and speak in public about matters regarded by most lay people as too high for their unaided understanding. And when a child is born, or a young man and woman decide to become engaged to be married, when serious illness or disaster visits a house or when death ruthlessly breaks in— at such times, not only in accordance with social convention, but also by a kind of only half-understood instinct, the help of a minister of religion is felt to be natural and desirable. By his ministration of the Sacraments, by his reminder of the great Christian promises and demands, by his prayers, spoken both in the name of God and of the Church, he can bring to these deeper experiences of life a sense of spiritual strength, comfort and hope. Such has been the traditional view of the functions of the ordained Ministry.

But in recent years, in the Western world, there has been discernible a change of attitude on the part of many people towards the parson and his particular role in society. The clergyman is undoubtedly something of an enigmatic figure (some would say, an anachronistic figure) in the social scene. As a contemporary writer puts it, "Most people no longer trust ministers, and are embarrassed in their presence. The average Englishman is still astonishingly kindly disposed towards the minister, and often treats him with great generosity and consideration. But this serves only to conceal the fact that he does not understand the minister, and has only the vaguest idea of what to expect from him."

It is true that the position of the clergyman in the community is unique. He belongs to no social class. He lives, or is expected to live, by different standards of value from those of the world or secular society. He takes no part in the 'rat race' of a materialistic and commercialised society. Generally speaking, his remuneration is regulated by need rather than professional ability, and his neighbours do not expect him to 'keep up with the Joneses'.

No less strange and different is his mode of life. For he has no regular 'working hours' except those comparatively few hours on Sundays or week-days when he can be counted upon to officiate at Divine Service, to preach, or to minister the Sacraments. The remainder of his time is entirely at his own disposal; and the use of it can vary vastly according to the nature of his parish, his temperament and gifts, and whether he is idle or industrious and conscientious.

Today, in some quarters, not only has the value of the clergyman's ministrations been questioned, but the very necessity of his office. This questioning is inspired by different considerations, some trivial, some more radical. There are many men and women, in this materialistic twentieth century, who feel little need of any reminder of spiritual realities and an unseen world. Others are critical of the whole conception of a distinction between the sacred and the secular. Others are suspicious of the very concept of priesthood, and see no need for any class of men ordained and set apart to speak on behalf of God or to interpret Scripture. Or again, many people today strongly question the desirability of a particular clerical class of men, living a life of comparative isolation from the tasks and tensions and temptations of ordinary life in the world of industry, trade and commerce. It is, I believe, this uncertainty about the vital value of an ordained minister which chiefly accounts for the tragic shortage of clergy today.

Such widespread doubts and questionings would seem to have the consequence of making the present task of the clergyman in society vastly more difficult and frustrating. Mr. Ludovic Kennedy, for example, spoke in a recent broadcast of "the rather lost feeling which a parson has at the present time —not knowing really what his identity is". Even a contemporary bishop has declared that "the parson's role in society becomes more and more uncertain".

There are other considerations tending in the same direction. For the twentieth-century world undoubtedly presents a somewhat new social and intellectual climate for the Christian minister to work in.

If Man himself, in his central needs and essential nature, does not greatly change from generation to generation, yet his environment changes and must affect his whole outlook. These changes must inevitably also affect the modern parson in all his work.

Perhaps the most important of these changes is that science

has replaced religion as the dominant influence in the realm of thought and education. Whereas in the Middle Ages the most familiar categories of thought were religious and philosophical, today they are scientific and technical. The new inventions and discoveries of our age have captivated the imagination of the man-in-the-street and are constantly adding both to the excitement and to the opportunities of life. Intelligent younger men and women today are more inclined to read books of science than of literature or philosophy. Even where religious literature is read with interest, the reader probably approaches it in a questioning and often sceptical frame of mind. Moreover, religion is no longer buttressed by custom or encouraged by conventional social sanctions. Whereas our grandparents often attended public worship under the constraint of respectability and displayed at least an outward reverence for the Church, the Bible and Christian ordinances, modern man feels no such constraints.

It is in fact no exaggeration to say that the Ministry in the twentieth century, alike in Europe and the Americas, has to be exercised in a semi-pagan society. Convinced and practising Christians are in a minority. A book published recently, *France Pagan*, shows how far these tendencies have already gone on the Continent. The writer describes certain industrial areas as "districts where no Christian tradition is left—love of money has devoured it, politics have ravished it, absence of the clergy has let it all die. No Christian life here, no Christian culture either. In this region, and in all like it, whether a man inhabits the elegant garden city or the vast workman's dwelling, he knows nothing of whence he comes, whither he is going, why he is on this earth. He has no reason for living, no guiding principles, no scale of values. Here we find nothing, sheer emptiness with civilisation superimposed."

Things may not be so serious with us in Britain. But it would probably be safe to say that, at least in certain of the large towns and in certain strata of society in our own country, Christian beliefs, customs and standards are scarcely taken any account of. It is well to face the somewhat harsh facts that the Church no longer exercises the authority and influence it once had; the Christian Faith no longer enjoys the intellectual status it once had; clergy no longer have the prestige and dignity they once had.

*   *   *

On the other hand, however, there are encouraging signs. Within thinking circles outside the Church there is a new interest both in spiritual values in general and in Christian beliefs in particular, discernible in much contemporary fiction, poetry, and painting.

Within the Church itself, the tide has turned from the vague religious humanism and the liberal outlook so popular twenty-five or thirty years ago to a renewed recognition of the value and spiritual authority of the Bible and Christian tradition, as witnesses to a unique Divine self-revelation in history. In spite of certain theological essays which have received exaggerated publicity and enjoyed a wide circulation, it looks as though there were among many younger people an unmistakable reaching out after the supernatural and transcendent. Admittedly this is only to be seen in very limited circles, but it is an extremely significant change. A series of lectures on Christian doctrine by Dr. J. S. Whale, delivered a few years ago in Cambridge, gathered audiences of five hundred or six hundred undergraduates.

Indeed, in spite of the domination of science, and in fact among many scientists themselves, there is a perceptible turning away from a purely materialistic view of life and of the universe. The same is true even, if only unconsciously, among many ordinary people. The Welfare State has brought many material benefits, which Christians should be the first to welcome. But there is a growing realisation that the provision of every comfort and convenience, which scientific research and technical skill make possible, is yet not solving the deepest human problems or supplying the deepest human needs. The strength and vitality of the new congregations established in new centres of population, with their overcrowded Sunday Schools and youth organisations, indicates a realisation that "man does not live by bread alone". This growing consciousness of spiritual need, dim and nebulous though it may often be, affords a more favourable climate for the exercise of the Christian Ministry.

It is sometimes suggested that the day of preaching is past; that in an age of universal education and excellent libraries and (comparatively) cheap books, there is no longer need for instruction or exhortation from a pulpit. I cannot agree. The Bible is a collection of writings little known among the vast majority of people; writings, many of which are difficult, requiring interpretation by a person trained in exegesis and theology. More than that, the great truths of the Christian Gospel gain greatly in force and appeal when proclaimed within the context of corporate worship and prayer. And it ought never to be forgotten (although, God forgive us, we preachers often do forget it) that the purpose of Christian preaching is not only instruction or exhortation but 'conversion', the persuasion of the hearers to turn in newness of faith and obedience to him who is "the Lord of all good life".

Perhaps the opportunity of the Christian preacher has never been greater or more exciting than today, when the Christian creed has to compete with so many rival philosophies and so many secular distractions. But if that is true, it is also true that the contemporary sermon must be prepared with the greatest care; that it must be spoken in both language and thought-forms natural to the age and the society in which we live; and that in choice of presentation of theme, it must be relevant to the needs and situations of our twentieth-century world. More than that, I believe that we need much more effective lines of communication between pulpit and pew; opportunities being afforded for genuine dialogue, for exchange of views and convictions, between the clergy and the laity—to the equal benefit of both sides!

There is another point in favour of the preacher today. As a result of the decline of merely conventional religious observance, the average congregation in church on Sundays is a much more spiritually satisfactory congregation. It consists almost entirely of people who have come not out of any sense of 'doing the proper thing', but because consciously or subconsciously they feel their need of God and of another dimension; or because they want to know a little more about what Christianity has to say; or because they are morally or spiritually lonely and feel that perhaps in the company of a Christian group they can find an answer to their spiritual isolation; or again, because they are puzzled and bewildered by the sheer mystery of life and its profounder experiences, and wonder if the Church has any real light to throw on these mysteries.

If I am at all right in this diagnosis of the situation, then the twentieth-century congregation on Sundays presents to the minister a stimulating, if somewhat terrifying, challenge and opportunity. In some cases we clergy are utterly inadequate to the challenge, and some in the congregation may go away disappointed and disillusioned, feeling that the prayers were unreal, the sermon dull and improperly prepared, or the atmosphere of the whole act of worship irrelevant to his or her own particular need and situation. At other times, by God's grace, the right word may have been spoken, the sense of true Christian brotherliness felt, and the person who was standing as it were on the edge of the crowd may be gradually drawn into the central warmth of the on-going life of the Christian community.

One thing is certain: amid all social changes, Man himself, in his innermost being and needs, does not really change. George Borrow tells of an Irish tinker woman who said to him: "O Sir, give us God! We need him, for we are a sinful people, and many is the sinful thing we have done." And when Borrow tried to escape by offering her money, she screamed after him: "We do not want your money, we have plenty of that. Give us God!"

"Give us God." That is the deepest need of man; the cry spoken or unspoken in the soul of every man. The whole vocation of the Christian Minister consists really in this one supreme task: to give men God; to make the reality of God clear to them; to make his majesty and love known to them. That is the impelling commanding motive of all he does: his preaching, his pastoral visiting, his prayers, his ministration of the Sacraments.

*   *   *

In the Church of Scotland, for many centuries, great stress has been laid upon the proclamation of 'the Word'. Indeed we have sometimes been accused of giving exaggerated prominence to the sermon. There is however ample biblical authority for this. St. Paul puts in the very foreground of the minister's calling the task of preaching. And he leaves us in no doubt as to what he believes should be the central note in preaching: "Unto me is this grace given that I should preach the unsearchable riches of Christ".

The Christian preacher is to point men to Christ. He is to introduce men to Christ. He is to speak of Christ in a hundred different situations: Christ in the home, Christ in the carpenter's shop, Christ in the sick room, Christ in the busy street, Christ teaching the crowds, Christ on the Cross, Christ coming out of the grave, Christ sitting at the right hand of God as

Great Intercessor, Christ still at work in the world. For Christianity proclaims that this same Christ is the supreme Revealer of God, the Agent of the Mighty Acts of God in history, and the only key to the meaning of this mysterious universe. The Stable, the Cross, the Empty Tomb, are windows that let us look into the very heart of Reality, and enable us to understand at least something of the meaning of life and suffering and struggle and death and human destiny beyond death.

It is because the Christian Gospel is a message which deals with those ultimate issues which confront Everyman that the Christian minister can proclaim it with confidence Sunday by Sunday, and carry it to men and women in their homes and who are fighting their own temptations, sorrows and problems.

We preachers are called to be ministers of "the Word"; God's Word in Christ. It is a Word that speaks to us in every department of human life and responsibility. Christ came to establish a new order of society, based on the sovereignty of God; and in his teaching and in his example we see the pattern of a new way of living. I believe in our own time there is a new sense of the relevance of Christianity to social problems; a new readiness to listen to what the Church has to say, on work and wages, on juvenile delinquency and prison reform, on colonial policy and race relationships, on disarmament, as seen in the light of the teaching of Jesus Christ.

Here is the great new challenge to the Church. And it means that the minister, however essential his reading and writing, dare not shut himself up in the rarified air of his study. He must also be involved in the wider life of the community. He must be in touch with men and women in the problems and tensions of everyday work. He must be alert to new movements of thought and new trends of behaviour. He must be prepared, if opportunity offers, to be an industrial chaplain, an army chaplain, or a school chaplain; welcoming the chance of entering unexpected doors and making new contacts, if only he is able to give men and women a glimpse of the vital relevance of the Christian Gospel. That is why the Christian minister today has discarded his long coat and top hat and ebony cane: symbols of status. Let us hope that he will not be persuaded, by arguments appealing to a specious modernity, to abandon the clerical collar, emblem of a special kind of service which the world will always need!

Looking back across more than thirty years in the Holy Ministry, one is conscious of mingled impressions and feelings. In spite of personal failures, inadequacies, disappointments, I can imagine no vocation that gives deeper satisfaction or richer rewards. And in this century of change and transition, if the demands made upon the Christian minister are greater, the challenge is the more exciting. We have to be ready for change and for experiment. We have to discriminate between the things that are of permanent and precious worth in the life and work of the Church and those that ought to be altered or abandoned. Re-thinking in the realm of liturgy may be necessary, in order to bring a new sense of meaningfulness and reality into corporate worship. Ancient words and time-honoured phrases may have to be re-interpreted if they are to become intelligible to a generation that no longer reads the Authorised Version of the Scriptures. The New English Bible is both a significant symbol and a potent instrument of this need for re-interpretation. The beauty of the Elizabethan English has been lost. Much of the sense of mystery and majesty has somehow vanished. But on the other hand the old documents have taken on a new freshness. They speak to people of this twentieth century with new power and relevance, and in an idiom that is more easily understood.

Only one thing is of fundamental importance in the proclamation of the Christian Gospel: namely that men and women shall listen and understand and believe and obey. Only one thing is of primary importance in public worship: namely that those taking part are enabled genuinely to pray, to hold converse with God. The constant concern of the parson must be, by whatever means, to accomplish these ends. The hymns he chooses, the vestments he uses, the ceremonial he devises (or discards), the sermons he composes, the parish activities he promotes, are all subservient to the one supreme purpose of helping to bring and to keep men in touch with God.

The grandeur of this purpose is the despair of those of us who are called to serve in the Holy Ministry. It is also our constant inspiration. And despite all our individual failures and despite all the vicissitudes of history, the living Church, under its eternal Lord, goes on.

FESTIVAL OF ST. KENTIGERN: 13TH JANUARY, 1965.

I. THE CHURCH IN AN AGE OF TRANSITION

THE VOCATION OF THE CHURCH

Moderatorial Address to the General Assembly of the Church of Scotland

Right Reverend and Right Honourable:

We live at a period in history when the Church is frequently criticised and even more frequently misunderstood. There are some who appear to think of it as an institution whose main purpose is to defend and propagate a certain set of theological dogmas. There are others who think of it as a kind of moral vigilance society, whose function is to propagate a somewhat puritanical code of ethics and condemn all who transgress against it. There are others who think of it rather as a large and venerable social club, in which the terms of membership are pleasantly nebulous, and in which people of many different tastes and backgrounds can find an atmosphere of friendliness and tolerance. Or again, there are others who conceive of the Church as a particular group of people who feel drawn to acts of piety, and, behind closed doors and in comfortably cushioned pews, sing rather sentimental hymns and listen to prayers and readings couched in an antique English never heard in any other place or context.

It is true that few of those who hold such views have any very intimate acquaintance with the Church, and seldom take part in its worship. But even more alarming perhaps is it that even within the membership of the Church there are those who are not very certain of its nature and its calling. In view of these misunderstandings and uncertainties, it is important that we should remind ourselves afresh from time to time what precisely is the vocation of the Christian Church; and that we should ask ourselves as honestly and as stringently as possible whether in our own day and generation we are fulfilling that vocation. It is to that question that I should like to ask you to devote our thought.

When we open the Scriptures of the New Testament, it becomes plain, alike in its every document, that the calling of the Christian Church involves two activities: A looking upwards to God in faith and expectation, and, on the other hand, a reaching outwards to the world in compassion and concern. In these two activities we see surely the perennial vocation of the Church. And by its obedience to this twofold calling it must be tested and judged at any given place or any given time in its history.

Obviously in such an attempted examination we are not to be concerned with other parts or branches of the Church catholic, but *are* to be concerned as honestly and humbly as possible with our own part of that Church and with our personal share in its successes or failures.

1. First then, is THE UPWARD LOOK OF THE CHURCH IN FAITH
   AND EXPECTANCY

Amongst the manifold and highly organised activities of the Church in this twentieth century, I think we are sometimes apt to forget that the Church is essentially a supernatural society; brought into being by God, sustained and empowered by God, and depending literally from moment to moment upon the grace of God. If it were otherwise, if it were simply a human institution, dependent merely upon the wisdom and efficiency of men, it would have perished long ago. Historians marvel not only at its survival but even more at the power of the impact which it has made upon the whole development of our Western civilisation. We who are Christians know that there is only one explanation: the Church derives its power from Above, from Beyond.

Now if that is so, then it must inevitably affect every aspect of the Church's life: indeed the whole attitude and method of the Church in carrying forward its mission. We do in fact see this very plainly in the earliest days. Dr. Karl Barth once said that the men and women who move across the pages of the New Testament seem like people who, every now and again, stop and look upwards as if in wonder and expectation. That is surely an almost perfect picture of what the Christian life should be: immersed in the ordinary business and affairs of this world, and yet keeping in constant touch with another unseen world, from which comes direction and spiritual strength.

Can we justly claim that this is the attitude of the Church in our own time? Or have we been so distracted by the dazzling

scientific achievements, the insidious claims of secular humanism, the rapid social changes amongst which we live, that we
have almost forgotten the need of the upward look? At least I
think we shall all agree that that is a temptation to be guarded
against.

For without this upward look, this sense of the Other
Dimension, the spiritual power and consequent spiritual
influence of the Church will be grievously diminished.

I sometimes have an uneasy suspicion that the very efficiency
of the Church of this twentieth century holds serious danger.
Because it is possible to mistake organisational efficiency for
spiritual power. Let us be honest: the Church in our land
today is not making the spiritual impact either upon the life
of the nation as a whole or upon the lives of individual men and
women that it should. Can we discern any reason for this
failure? I believe the answer lies in a single sentence: We are not
looking upwards as we ought in humble faith and expectation.
For something of the secularism of the age has invaded the
Church.

This looking upward in faith and expectation expresses
itself supremely in prayer.

Prayer is the main line of communication between the Church
on earth and the world of heavenly or eternal reality. Worship
and prayer are therefore, or ought to be, the primary activities
of the Church. Alike in its acts of corporate worship and through
private acts of devotion by its individual members, the Church
is constantly seeking and receiving help from Above and
Beyond. Yes, because *there* is the Source, the inexhaustible
Source of the Church's power.

Yet it is perhaps at this very point that there lies the greatest
weakness in the life of our Scottish Church today. We have a
well-educated body of clergy. We have a devoted band of
Elders and Deacons, Deaconesses and workers. We are engaged
in many valuable and beneficent enterprises. We are alert to
the need of evangelism in a semi-pagan society. Our ecclesiastical machinery runs, on the whole, with admirable efficiency
and smoothness. No one, listening to the reports and debate
of the General Assembly, could fail to be impressed by the
range of the Church's interest and concern.

Yet among our multifarious activities, prayer is apt to be
crowded out, and its importance forgotten. To many people

I suspect that the part of Divine Worship on Sundays which appears to have least reality and relevance are the devotions. It is significant that, while fifty years ago, a week-day prayer meeting was held in the vast majority of parishes, today it is almost unknown. At a farewell gathering of parishioners recently held in his honour, a well-loved Minister said that, as he looked back across the years, one of the things he most keenly regretted was that he had allowed the prayer meeting to be abandoned. In few homes today are family prayers ever said. Even that simplest of all forms of religious observance, grace before meals, is fallen largely into disuse. Yet prayer is the chief source of the Church's spiritual power.

Useful discussion takes place in many youth groups and 'brains trusts' about Christian doctrine. And it is one of the healthier signs of the times that people are more ready than formerly to talk about religion in all kinds of unexpected places. Yet discussion *about* God is no substitute for converse *with* God. It was Martin Luther who said: "As a shoemaker makes a shoe and a tailor makes a coat, so ought a Christian to pray. Prayer is the daily business of a Christian."

If this is true of every practising Christian, how particularly true is it of those of us who are called to the Holy Ministry! I will only quote here some searching words spoken by the late Evelyn Underhill:

"Prayer, for the Minister of religion, is the unique source of pastoral power . . . Other things—intellectual and social aptitudes, good preaching, a capacity for organisation—help his work, and help much. None of these, however, is essential. Prayer is. The man whose life is coloured by prayer, whose loving communion with God comes first, will always win souls; because he shows them in his own life and person the attractiveness of reality, the demand, the transforming power of the spiritual life . . . It follows from this, that the Minister's life of prayer, his communion with God, is not only his primary obligation to the Church; it is also the only condition under which the work of the Christian Ministry can be properly done . . . The business of the Christian Minister is to lead men out towards eternity; and how can he do this unless it is a country in which he is at home?"[1]

[1] *Mixed Pasture.* By kind permission of Methuen & Co. Ltd.

If a personal reference may be forgiven; looking back across the years of my own Ministry, crowded with activity (often too crowded) I am grievously conscious that one thing has been lacking. I have not contrived to make sufficient spaces for quiet, for prayer and meditation and 'waiting upon God'.

This upward look in faith and expectation is no less vitally important in the task of preaching.

We who are called to proclaim the Word of God need constantly to remember that preaching is essentially a supernatural activity. Utterly different in character from the speaking of the university lecturer instructing his students, or the Member of Parliament addressing his constituents, or the poet reciting his verse, or the explorer describing his travels. Because in all these cases, the determinative element is the learning or the eloquence or the charm or the creative imagination of the speaker. But preaching is, or ought to be, essentially supernatural in character; dependent for its efficacy, not upon the eloquence or the learning or even the personality of the preacher, but upon the wisdom and power that come 'from above'.

An eminent church dignitary was staying with some friends in the country. When strolling in the garden one day, he came upon the small daughter of the house sitting on her swing. They got into conversation. Suddenly the little girl shot a somewhat unexpected question at him: "I can see God when I sit here on my swing. Do you see God from your pulpit?" A highly pertinent question. Because unless he, the preacher, sees God as he stands in his pulpit, and unless the people through him hear the voice of God, his sermons are not likely to be very effectual. Indeed, that is possibly one reason why much preaching today seems to make little spiritual impact upon the hearers. From a literary or an academic point of view, it may be admirable. It may be possible to hold the interest of a congregation by apt topical reference or vivid illustration or intelligent argument. But such rhetorical devices, however pleasing, are not the important thing. The essential thing in true preaching, which marks it off from all other forms of human speech, is the upward look of the preacher, in humble faith and expectancy; so that his own poor words, infused with divine power, become the Word of God. Men and women will recognise such preaching when they hear it.

Old Dr. Zachary Boyd, in his *Last Battell of the Soul*, has a striking reminder for all of us preachers: "My sermons must be read before Him that sent me to preach; for Hee will know how I have fedde His Lambes."

There is one aspect of this matter which I believe deserves particular consideration; I mean the place of prayer and devotion in the training for the Holy Ministry. We in Scotland have for long, and rightly, prided ourselves on the high academic standard set for the education of our clergy. That standard is, I think, universally regarded with respect, and in some quarters with envy. Such academic equipment is more important than ever in contemporary society, where the general level of education is relatively high, and where the minister of religion has to be ready effectively to commend and defend the Christian Faith and Ethic, whether against sceptics or against adherents of rival creeds and philosophies.

Yet, while all that is true, I dare to suggest that our traditional preparation for the Holy Ministry is too exclusively intellectual. Theology is no mere academic discipline like philosophy. It calls not only for intellectual ability but for humble faith. The student of Divinity must be constantly looking upwards for the illumination of the Holy Spirit, no less than to the expert instruction of his tutors. Looking back in memory to my own years in the study of Divinity, I can recall that, along with profound gratitude for the ripe scholarship of distinguished teachers, so freely and generously made available, there was also in the minds of many of us the consciousness of something lacking in the life of the college: an attitude of awe and wonder evoked by a sense of the 'numinous', a recognition of the majesty, the holiness, the demandingness of God. Nor does that situation seem greatly to have changed. For, during the last ten or fifteen years, Divinity students from all the colleges have from time to time spoken to me of this same kind of impression.

With great respect, I suggest that there is need for more guidance in the spiritual life and more encouragement to devotion: more opportunities for consultation about problems of the inner life; more spaces in the time-table set aside both for corporate prayer and for private meditation.

The Rev. Charles Walker has recently reminded us that some of the profoundest Christian thinkers, such as St. Thomas Aquinas, St. Anselm, and John Calvin, were no less spiritually devout than intellectually brilliant:

"Diverse in time, and dissimilar in the direction of their talents, all three were alike in this, that they loved God with their minds and with their hearts, and probably gave as much time and thought to prayer as to speculation."

More than that, I believe that there is urgent need for at least one residential theological college, at which every student of Divinity would spend not less than a full session: a college in which there would be some simple pattern of devotional discipline, and in which the centre and focus of the life of the whole community would be the chapel, with its regular acts of worship, morning and evening, its gatherings round the Lord's Table, its atmosphere of silence and serenity encouraging private prayer. Theological studies in such a setting would be infused with a new warmth and reverence and vitality. And men going out from such a community to the active Ministry would carry with them a sense not only of the sacredness but of the infinite spiritual resources of their calling.

In this connection, I must refer to one matter which may seem at first sight superficial, but which in fact has profound significance: I mean the spectacle of the doors of the great majority of churches in Scotland closed and barred on week-days. The justification of this custom is frequently said to lie in the conviction that no one building is more sacred than another, and that those who desire to pray can do so in their own room. So to argue is to ignore both social and psychological realities. There are a great many houses, in both town and countryside, where no quiet and privacy can be secured for prayer and meditation, and where conditions of family life are such that silence is almost unknown. Apart from the multifarious necessary domestic activities, in thousands of homes today the wireless or television set fills the air with the sound of voices or music from early afternoon until night.

In such circumstances, a church can provide one of the few places in our noise-haunted modern world where an atmosphere of peace is to be found. It is a place moreover "where prayer is wont to be made", a building which has been erected for the single purpose of promoting converse between God and man, and in which probably for generations, possibly for centuries, men and women have come to honour God and lift their minds to eternal realities.

This is true of even the plainest church, with little architectural beauty or splendour. For its very furnishings speak, silently but unmistakably, to all who enter in any spirit of reverence: the pulpit and lectern proclaiming that God speaks to us men, and that in his Word those who are willing to listen will find comfort and challenge and guidance; the Holy Table proclaiming that God reaches out towards us men, offering us in the Sacrament the Bread of Life to sustain and strengthen us in our spiritual weakness; the rows of pews reminding us that the Christian Life is meant to be no solitary business, but life within the warm fellowship of a great family, "the household of faith".

After long generations of contrary custom, I do not suggest that it will be easy to persuade our Scottish folk to think once again of the parish church as a place in which it is natural to turn for peace to pray. It may take many years, and require much teaching and preaching. But I believe that if ministers and Kirk Sessions will decide, even in face of risk or of scepticism, to keep churches open daily, it will not only help to create the climate of prayerfulness so urgently needed in the religious life of contemporary Scotland, but will also serve to suggest that religion is a business not for one day but for seven days in the week.

*　　　*　　　*

There has been evident in recent years, if not a deep longing for spiritual revival, yet at least a recognition that such a spiritual revival is greatly needed. More than one attempt has been made to prepare for and create conditions for such a revival; but without noticeable success. And the reason is plain: not the most efficient organisation, or the most elaborate planning or the most eloquent preaching, can bring about spiritual revival in the land. It must come from above.

May it be that one thing has been lacking? We have not looked upward sufficiently in expectation? The fundamental preparation is prayer, and we have not given ourselves enough to prayer. We have not even *believed* enough in prayer! In the earliest days the Christian Church was essentially an expectant Church. It was to the community waiting in prayer and expectation in an upstairs room on the Day of Pentecost that the Holy Spirit came in indescribable power. If the Church in our land becomes in fuller degree a praying Church and an expectant Church, then there may be granted to us such a fresh outpouring of the Holy Spirit as will bring us that dynamic revival and renewal for which we long.

*   *   *

2. But if the primary task of the Church is the upward look to God in faith and expectation, no less important is the OUTWARD LOOK TOWARDS THE WORLD IN COMPASSION AND CONCERN.

This outreach of the Church towards the world finds of course its first and most obvious expression in the attempt to proclaim and win a hearing for the Gospel among those who have scarcely yet heard it, or who until now have turned a deaf ear to its appeal. We are living in days of unusual challenge and opportunity. New nations are being born. Backward peoples are achieving independence and political responsibility. The arrogant philosophy of Communism is increasing its empire with terrifying rapidity and ruthlessness. More insidious but perhaps scarcely less dangerous is the growth of Secular Humanism, encouraged and fortified by the amazing achievements of science and technology. And as a consequence and concomitant of these various movements, almost everywhere there is a revolt against traditional religious beliefs and moral standards.

Is it any cause for wonder that modern Man, buffeted and distracted by these 'winds of change', appears often to have lost his bearings; seeing no longer any sign-posts to guide him, and possessing no standards of value to enable him to make sound judgments as to the philosophies and ideologies clamouring for his attention.

It is in such a climate that the Church in our time is called to fulfil its vocation. Never has the need for the sustaining power of the Christian Gospel been more obviously urgent. But seldom can it have been more difficult to obtain a hearing for that Gospel or to find means of proclaiming it in terms which Modern Man can understand.

Yet this great task of evangelism, in spite of every obstacle and frustration, remains the primary vocation of the Church.

This outward thrust of the Christian Church into the very strongholds of Islam, Hinduism, Buddhism in other lands, through the centuries, has been an astonishing venture of faith, not only demanding physical and moral courage of the highest order, but also implying an indomitable confidence in its own message that Jesus Christ is indeed the Light of the World and the Saviour of Mankind. Against all human probabilities of success, and in spite of every frustration and hazard, this great enterprise goes on, and must go on, in obedience to the Master's own command to "preach the Gospel to every creature".

But this outward reach of the Church in evangelism must find expression also within our own country. Careful and objective investigation has shown that here in Scotland there are tens of thousands of men, women and children who have no association of any sort with the Church, except perhaps that which manifests itself in an occasional request for Christian marriage or baptism; thousands of homes in which the name of God is never spoken, no Christian customs observed, and the children grow up unbaptised. The seriousness of the situation is such that certain acute observers have even suggested that in Europe we are living in what might be called a Post-Christian era.

Here is a challenge to the Church which until now, although we have begun to recognise it, we have not fully faced. I believe that, so far as our own country is concerned, it can only be met on certain conditions.

(a) The first condition is that we attempt in our church life to make the parochial system a reality. I am aware that recently it has been said that the parochial system is no longer evangelically effective, and is in fact out of date. I venture to question that. In a country like our own, where there is a recognised National Church, the operation of the parish pattern is not only possible but presents potentialities of great value. The ecclesiastical partitioning of Scotland into parishes carries with it the implication that a Minister and Kirk Session are responsible for the spiritual shepherding and care of every man, woman and child in the land. Now in theory this is a splendid conception and ideal; but in practice, it is tragically neglected. It is true that the comfort of the Word and Sacrament are available for all who desire it; the doors of the Church are open in invitation to all who are prepared to enter; the minister is accessible to all in the parish who need his counsel. And we can be deeply thankful that in these respects the parochial ideal is partially achieved, whether in the densely populated industrial areas or in the small islands of the Western and Northern seas.

But that is not enough. If the parochial system is a reality, then it implies a deep concern that every man, woman and child within the parish shall be brought to *accept* the Gospel, and use the Sacraments, and join in the worship of the Lord's House on the Lord's Day. But, perhaps partly due to the almost intolerable pressures of modern life, we are in danger of losing sight of that responsibility. The unit of ecclesiastical concern is too often the congregation rather than the parish; the relatively converted and faithful whose names are on the Roll of Communicants, not the careless, the indifferent, the lapsed, the hostile. The parish minister is expected to expend most of his pastoral thought and energy upon the members of his own faithful flock. And if he conscientiously fulfils their expectations, he will in most cases have little time or strength left to seek out the heedless, the bewildered, the lost. Until somehow we remedy this failure to operate the parochial system by such an outreach of concern towards the churchless, we shall make little impact upon the life of the nation as a whole.

(*b*) Which leads us to the second condition. For this outreach towards the lapsed and the indifferent cannot be made unless congregations show a new spirit of unselfishness and understanding; encouraging the parish minister to put the needs of the unconverted and the careless before those of professing and practising Christians. When that happens, many of the clergy will feel able to use their time and strength in very different ways, and will perhaps be seen, like their Master, frequently in the company of publicans and sinners. Studdert Kennedy, for example, beloved Army Chaplain 'Woodbine Willie' of the First War, usually spent his Saturday evenings in Worcester in various public houses, talking to men who seldom entered a church. A strange, but strangely effective, mode of evangelism!

With any influence which a speaker from this Moderatorial Chair may possess, I would entreat the faithful church people of Scotland to release their minister from his constant pastoral attention to *them*, in order that instead he may go into the highways and byways and visit the homes of the careless, the indifferent, the hostile; whether it be in cottage or castle, in the country villages or in the overcrowded streets and tenements of great cities; seeking those who never voluntarily place themselves within reach of the Word and the Sacraments.

(*c*) The third condition of any success in this great task of evangelism in our country is the recognition of the responsibility of laymen and women.

In most branches of the Church it has traditionally been assumed that the winning of men and women to the Christian Faith was the task of the clergy; and that in the enterprise of evangelism the pulpit was the chief if not the sole instrument. In countries or in periods of history when the great majority of the population attended church, although often under the pressure of ecclesiastical sanctions or of public opinion, opportunities of direct evangelism by the preaching of the Word were of course considerable.

But certainly those conditions no longer prevail in Britain today. Great numbers of the people scarcely ever enter a place of worship, and so never hear the preaching of the Gospel. Moreover the number of men offering themselves for the Ministry of our own Church is still tragically inadequate.

Here is the challenge to the Christian laity to recognise their responsibility and to play their part.

It is impossible to suggest here in any detail what that part should be. Many possibilities will disclose themselves. Adventurous experiment in many different directions is called for. Already indeed such new ventures are being attempted: the house church, the congregational mission, parish enterprises, the Iona Community, Kirk Week, 'Group Workshops'.

The "Stewardship and Budget Campaigns" being planned at present in many congregations are particularly full of promise, and have revealed to many ordinary Christian lay-folk the romance and exhilaration of working for the Kingdom of Christ in our tormented and disillusioned twentieth-century world.

But the greatest potential lies still in the Eldership; that immense body of men, drawn from countless different trades and professions, with endlessly diverse gifts and abilities, distributed from end to end across the country. It is the envy of many other Communions: thousands of laymen publicly committed to the service of the Church and the furtherance of the Christian cause.

Yet is this institution of the Eldership being used to the full

in the re-Christianising of contemporary Scotland? Is it playing
as dynamic a part as it might? I ask these questions, very humbly
and respectfully, yet sincerely. I ask them rather than dare to
try and answer them.

One thing is certain: that if lay people are to take a greater
share in the task of evangelism, they must be far better instructed in the great doctrines of the Christian Faith and in the
history of the Church. Under the pressures of modern life and
under the enormously powerful impact of the cinema, broadcasting, television, and the popular press with its newspapers
and magazines, the traditional Scottish interest in theology has
diminished. But there are welcome signs, in many quarters, that
men and women desire to know 'what Christianity has to say'.

Instructed laymen, and especially office-bearers, can play a
valuable part in answering such questions, if they themselves
have conviction and knowledge. Opportunities may present
themselves in all kinds of unexpected situations, perhaps in
casual conversation in the homes of friends and acquaintances,
in workshop or office. I think for example of a young man who
had embarked upon a career in banking. He told me that he had
been so impressed by the qualities of character and Christian
conviction manifested in the manager of the branch where he
was employed, that some two years later he decided to enter a
Divinity Hall, with a view to ordination to the Holy Ministry.

One of the most exciting and promising of recent developments in the preparation of the laity has been the setting up of
a committee on Adult Christian Education. Already, up and
down the country, it has been able to organise courses of instruction which have been attended by a large number of Elders
drawn from every different walk of life. With a somewhat
different approach, the recently opened St. Ninian's House at
Crieff is training younger men and women in techniques of
evangelism. It is along such lines and many others that the
Church must reach outwards in compassion and concern
towards those who still have little touch with God and spiritual
realities.

But if the Gospel is to be communicated to the men and women
of our time, a new vocabulary must be found. Here is perhaps the
hardest part of the preacher's task in the modern world, and one
which few of us have even begun to master. Yet, unless we can
somehow translate the traditional language of the pulpit into

the simple, direct, sometimes absurd, language of the teenager in the dance-hall, the worker in the shipyard, or the journalist in his newspaper column, we need not hope to win their interest, far less their allegiance and commitment to him who is the Lord of all good life.

A few months ago a very significant conversation, presented on television, took place in a studio of the British Broadcasting Corporation, between an eminent Church dignitary and a popular young pop singer. Adam Faith declared, before an unseen audience of probably ten or twelve million people, that he believed in God and religion. But, he went on to declare, he found the church services, alike in sermons and hymns, both irrelevant and unreal. They did not 'register' at all. They gave him nothing. Here is one of the plainest and most urgent challenges to the Church in our time, and one which cannot be ignored, except at the possible cost of losing a whole generation of young men and women to the ranks of the Christian cause.

*   *   *

I have spoken chiefly of the concern and outreach of the Church towards the world in terms of evangelism. Because the Gospel of Jesus Christ is the most precious thing which the Church has to offer. But the Church does not truly fulfil its calling unless it feels and shows concern for men and women in the whole range of their lives; in their material, no less than their spiritual welfare, in all their varied needs and responsibilities and relationships. It must encourage all that makes it easier for men to achieve fulfilment, physically, mentally and spiritually. It must not hesitate to protest against injustice wherever it shows itself, against exploitation of any group in the community, against any infringement of human rights, whether based on class or race.

There have been periods in its history when this concern was largely lacking. There can be no doubt that during parts of the eighteenth and nineteenth centuries when the Industrial Revolution brought catastrophic changes in the social structure and ways of life of multitudes of humbler people, the Church alike in England and in Scotland lost the trust of vast numbers of those engaged in industry, because of its apparent lack of concern for the moral and material welfare of the workers. The consequence was a bitter harvest of distrust in the Church, which in some degree is still with us today, especially in the cities and larger towns, and causes a major problem in the task of evangelism.

Yet, generally speaking, through the centuries the Church has a noble record of social concern. And in our own time and in our own country that concern is perhaps keener and more alert than it has ever been. Social science has demonstrated how great an influence environment has upon character and development of personality. If that be so, then the Church in its outreach towards men and women must show concern for all that conditions or affects their well-being: the surroundings in which they live, the conditions in which they work, the recreations they enjoy, the family problems they have to face, and indeed the whole structure and pattern of the life of the nation. As has been truly said: "What is necessary is corporate Christian thinking about the whole life of the community; and this Christians are doing, perhaps as never before."

Let us give no heed to those voices which declare that the Church must keep to its own domain; that it may concern itself with the solemn Coronation of a queen, but take no concern for the wages of a crossing-sweeper; that it may encourage the satisfactory singing of hymns on Sunday, but not the satisfactory using of tools on Monday; that it should have something to say to the devout worshipper in his pew, but need have nothing to say to the scientist in his laboratory or the financier in his board-room, the journalist in his newspaper office or the politician in the council chamber.

The plain fact is that the demand for the Church to confine its interest and its influence to its own domain is completely irrelevant. For the proper domain of the Church is the whole arena of human life; and the outreach of the Church in sympathy and concern is towards men and women in every situation or predicament or relationship.

This concern may compel it at times to intervene in what appear to be purely political or economic or cultural issues. But when it so intervenes, it is because the moral and spiritual welfare of the individual or of the community is at stake. And a Church that hesitates at such times or on such issues to speak plainly and fearlessly is failing in its vocation. When and how to speak on public questions is a problem demanding most careful thought and humble prayer; and even thereafter, as we well know in the General Assembly, it may be difficult to reach agreement! Nevertheless, the Church, as a Church, must at least make manifest its concern for righteousness, justice and truth in the whole life of the nation.

* * *

What I have been trying to do is to remind you, as I would remind myself, that the vocation of the Church is to be found in two directions: love of God and love of men. If ever the Church is tempted to forget either of these, the whole balance and perspective of its life is distorted, it can only truly minister to the deepest needs of men if it keeps constant converse with God. Because everything that it has to give men, whether through Word or Sacrament or in spiritual guidance and comfort, it itself receives from God.

The Church, if it is to exert its proper influence and make its unique contribution to the life of the nation and the world, must be the Church. Not a voluntary society with a kindly humanitarian outlook and an idealistic philosophy, not a powerful organisation, making its impact upon society by its able leaders, its efficient methods of recruitment, its streamlined structure of administration, its valuable 'contacts', its venerable history and traditions. If we rely upon such things, if we hold such a conception of the Church, then the acids of secularism will inevitably poison the life of the Christian community, and sap its spiritual strength.

The Church must be the Church. It must know itself to be no man-made institution, but a divine society. It must recognise that ultimately it depends for success not upon its efficiency but upon its faith; not upon the human weapons it forges by its own skill, but upon the spiritual weapons made available to it from an Unseen Arsenal. It must know that, faced by the mighty forces of evil and unbelief, it has no sufficiency of its own; but that, looking upwards in expectancy, it can count upon complete sufficiency in the invincible power and grace of God.

C

ONE CHURCH OR MANY CHURCHES?

"There is one body and one Spirit, as there is also one hope held out in God's call to you; one Lord, one faith, one baptism; one God and Father of all, who is over all and through all and in all."

Ephesians 4: 4-6[1]

"For just as in a single human body there are many limbs and organs, all with different functions, so all of us, united with Christ, form one body, serving individually as limbs and organs to one another."

Romans 12: 5

There can be little doubt that when the religious history of the twentieth century comes to be written, the drawing closer together of long-separated Christian churches in friendship and understanding will be seen as the most significant fact. The Ecumenical Movement, inevitably slow and tentative in its beginnings, has in recent years displayed more definitely the characteristics of 'movement'. The concept of Reunion has begun to capture the imagination of an increasing number of Christian people in many lands. Divisions, suspicions, rivalries, long accepted as natural in church life, are now recognised if not as sinful, yet certainly as deplorable.

There is however still a very long way to be travelled before any sort of reunion becomes possible; and a great deal of serious and honest thinking about the issues involved is needed, not only on the part of professional theologians and ecclesiastical leaders, but on the part of ordinary Christian people in all the different communions.

Perhaps, especially, we need more thinking about the doctrine of the Church, its nature and calling. Because all 'conversations' between those of different denominations and traditions really hinge on this central fundamental question: What *is* the Church?

[1] All New Testament quotations are taken from the *New English Bible, New Testament*, copyright 1961, by permission of Oxford and Cambridge University Presses.

If, greatly daring, one were to try and answer that question in a single simple sentence, the answer should probably be something like this: The Church is the family of all baptised persons who acknowledge Jesus Christ as God and Saviour. That, it seems to me, is the conception of the Church which we find in the writings of the New Testament. If we adopt any narrower conception than that, then we are in danger of drawing up frontiers different from those which we see in the New Testament. In the book of Acts we are told that at the end of the first Christian sermon ever preached, and listened to by a great crowd in the open-air, the people asked the preacher, St. Peter: "What are we to do?" And at once came the answer: "Repent and be baptised, every one of you, in the name of Jesus the Messiah". Baptism and belief in Christ: these are the fundamental marks of the Church.

In that ancient document which is accepted throughout a very large part of Christendom, the Nicene Creed, the Church is described by four adjectives: "I believe in One Holy Catholic and Apostolic Church."

In any discussions about reunion each of those words is of cardinal importance. And at the present time, if we are to be qualified to form any wise judgments about the relation of our own Communion to others, it is essential that we should try to be clear as to what it is that we mean when we talk about the Church as one, holy, catholic and apostolic. May we then think very briefly about each of these adjectives in turn.

I. THE UNITY OF THE CHURCH

There can be no doubt whatsoever that in the New Testament writings it is assumed that the Church is one. Jesus our Lord in his great prayer with his disciples just before his death, prayed, "May they all be one: as thou, Father, art in me, and I in thee, so also may they be one in us." So St. Paul in his Letter to the Romans, writes: "Just as in a single human body there are many limbs and organs, all with different functions, so all of us, united with Christ, form one body, serving individually as limbs and organs to one another." And in his Letter to the Ephesians: "There is one Body and Spirit, as there is also one hope held out in God's call to you; one Lord, one faith, one baptism, one God and Father of all."

The unity of the Church, that is to say, is not a thing contrived by any human arrangement. It derives from Christ. The Church consists of men and women and children who have been grafted into Christ by Baptism, and who are bound to Christ by loyalty and love. It is this shared baptism and belief, this intimate relationship to Jesus Christ, which brings them by that very fact, and in spite of all differences, into an intimate relationship with one another. So that all Christians as such are members of a single family. In a very real sense, therefore, the unity of the Church is a given fact, which can neither be denied nor in its inner essence destroyed.

2. THE HOLINESS OF THE CHURCH

This word presents difficulty to many people. Because so obviously the Church as we know it seems to be anything but holy. On the contrary, it is stained by pride and prejudice, by worldliness and pomposity, by indifference and sloth.

But the word 'holy', as used in the New Testament and as used in the Creeds does not mean morally good or spiritually perfect. It means 'belonging to God', consecrated to God's glory and for God's service. In so far as we sometimes forget that, and think of the Church as an end in itself, a kind of pleasant religious society or club existing for its own purposes, we have completely departed from the New Testament conception of the Church. The Church is holy, because it belongs to God and exists simply in order to glorify God and fulfil his purposes. It is in the same sense that, in the New Testament, the members of the Church are constantly referred to as 'Saints'.

3. THE CATHOLICITY OF THE CHURCH

Perhaps no word in the religious vocabulary has been abused more than this, and it leads to many misunderstandings between different branches of the Church. It is sometimes contrasted with the word 'Protestant'. It is sometimes used to describe a particular ecclesiastical party or to describe those who hold to a particular set of doctrines and traditions. One great branch of the Church indeed claims that it alone *is* the Catholic Church. It is ironical that those who use the word in such ways are frequently the most narrow and exclusive in their ecclesiastical outlook!

Whereas 'catholic' actually means 'universal, all-embracing'. When we profess belief in the catholic Church, we implicitly acknowledge that the family of God is not confined to those of any one race or nation, not confined to those of any one theological school or ecclesiastical tradition, but embraces all baptised persons who acknowledge Jesus Christ as God and Saviour. That is the biblical conception of the Church. "Whoever calls upon the name of the Lord shall be saved."

In any conversations about reunion it is of the utmost importance that this great word should be used not in any narrow or limiting sense but in its grand all-embracing sense. We can only begin to understand and respect and trust one another when we recognise one another as all alike belonging to the one catholic Church.

4. THE APOSTOLICITY OF THE CHURCH

"I believe in one holy catholic apostolic Church."

The Christian Church is not an institution which came into being by the desire or intention or planning of certain religiously minded people. It is an institution which was brought into being as the result of a particular set of happenings at a particular moment in history: the life and death and resurrection of Jesus Christ. In these happenings something new came into the process of history. God manifested in Christ as never before his power and compassion.

The Church came into being primarily in order to proclaim Christ, his life and teaching, his death and resurrection, and to go on proclaiming that message through the centuries. He himself had chosen a small group of men to be the first to proclaim it: the Apostles. They knew him; they had talked and walked with him; had seen him in all kinds of situations; had listened to him preaching. They were the natural first leaders of the Church, trusted and honoured beyond all others.

When we say that the Church is apostolic, we say that it goes back in unbroken continuity to those first leaders chosen by our Lord Himself; and that the true test of its life and worship, its witness and teaching must always be its loyalty to the truth and the way of Christian life as first proclaimed by the Apostles.

At least the fundamentals of their teaching and practice are recorded in the Bible. Hence the importance that the Church of England, the Church of Scotland and other Churches alike, especially since the Reformation, have attributed to Holy Scripture. By its teaching, which we believe to be the teaching of the Apostles, we test all that is done and believed in the Church.

It is through this continuity of the Church's life and witness from the Apostles onward, through a duly authorised Ministry and by the preaching of the Word and observance of the Sacraments, that the purity of the Church is maintained. And it is for each branch of the Church from time to time to examine alike its doctrine and order, its customs and traditions, humbly and honestly in the light of apostolic teaching and practice, so far as we can discern them in the pages of Holy Scripture.

Here then is the doctrine of the Church and its chief marks. This doctrine must underlie all ecumenical conversations.

Yet there are still people who ask, Why should we desire the reunion of the separated branches of the Church?

Why should we not be content to continue in our own denominational traditions and loyalties, provided that we are tolerant and charitable towards others?

Well, the first, and the most weighty, answer is that in the New Testament unity seems plainly to be regarded as of the very essence of the Christian Church. Jesus as we have seen prayed for his disciples, "May they all be one: as Thou Father art in me, and I in Thee; so also may they be in us, that the world may believe that Thou didst send me."

The Church is described by St. Paul as the household or family of God. In another place it is described as the 'Body of Christ.' Wherever a household or family is living as it should, it is united, its members living together in affection and trust and understanding. The second metaphor suggests even closer and more intimate unity, for a body is an organism; and if it is healthy, all its members function in complete harmony one with another. In the New Testament then, the Church is clearly thought of as one.

The Church as we know it today has somehow lost this essential unity. With the passing of the centuries, differences of belief and worship and custom crept in. And these differences led to schism and division. So that today as we look out across the world, or even across our own land, we see not one Church but many Churches; Roman Catholic, Presbyterian, Anglican, Congregationalist, Baptist. And almost inevitably misunderstanding, rivalries, resentments, prejudices are born. So that different Christians as it were dig themselves in to their own positions, cling to their own customs, pride themselves on their own ways of doing things. The harmony of the household of God has been shattered. Understanding, sympathy, trust have been undermined. And, most tragic of all, Christians can no longer all sit down together at the Lord's Table.

If, in any household, differences of outlook and conviction as between its members are allowed to lead to such rivalry and rancour, such misunderstanding and distrust that they can no longer talk together frankly, eat together happily, and enjoy one another's company—then the unity of the family has been spoiled, its common life disrupted. And everything possible must be done to break down the divisions and separations by the exercise of charity, until it leads to healing and reconciliation, even at a great cost on both sides.

That is exactly the situation in the Christian family, the Church, as we know it today. Although it is a family and nothing can destroy its fundamental, spiritual unity, yet that unity has been grievously damaged. It is no longer a visible unity. Differences of outlook and tradition have been allowed to lead to rivalry and rancour, misunderstanding and distrust, between certain of its members. So that they can no longer enjoy one another's company in worship or prayer, no longer talk together frankly on the great questions of our common faith, no longer sit down together at our Lord's own Table. If that is so, then everything possible must be done to break down the divisions and separations by the exercise of charity, by readiness to try and understand the point of view of others, until it leads to healing and reconciliation even at a great cost on both sides. At a great cost: because there is no easy road to reunion. It is a road that will inevitably demand from those who are brave enough to travel it, humility, patience, and readiness for sacrifice. But there is no other way. And the alternative is increasing stagnation and isolation. As the Archbishop of Canterbury has said: "The Church that lives to itself will die by itself."

There is another reason why we are called to seek closer unity: namely because a divided Church can only give a dis-

torted witness to the world. If there is one weakness in the life
of the Christian Church which above all others gives scandal
and brings dishonour upon it, it is these divisions and disagree-
ments among Christians. "If there is this love among you, then
all will know that you are my disciples," said Jesus. How often
we have allowed denominational pride and prejudice to stifle
charity! A Church disrupted by jealousies and suspicions cannot properly proclaim the Gospel of reconciliation. The man-
in-the-street, the outsider, is bewildered, astonished, often
shocked by all the different Christian labels. Almost certainly
large numbers of men and women refuse to come into the
Church because of its 'unhappy divisions.' And if that is true in
our own country, it is much more true in the mission-field. I
remember hearing an Indian Christian at an ecumenical
conference ask bluntly, "Why have you brought your Western
denominational differences to my country, where they mean
nothing, and only cause confusion?" At the present time certain
educated Hindus, sympathetic to Christian belief, are holding
back from joining the Christian Church because of its divisions.

There is a second question which many people are asking:
If we are to seek closer unity among the churches, what kind
of unity is it to be?

One thing is, surely, plain from the New Testament: it is to
be a visible unity. Mere tolerance and charity as between the
different denominations is not enough. St. Paul says: "There is
one body and one Spirit." This would seem at least to imply
that Christians living in the same country and the same town
should all be recognisably members of the one household of
God; free to worship together, to pray together, to receive the
Sacrament together; people who recognise Jesus Christ as their
common Lord and Saviour, people who accept the same Baptism, profess the same faith, recognise the same ministerial
order, live under the same spiritual discipline.

But while we are called to work and pray for the recovery of
the visible unity of the Church, it must not be a unity that means
uniformity. Rigid uniformity in worship, for example, would
be a loss and not a gain to the Church. God has made men and
women different in taste and temperament. He has set us in
different lands where history has brought diverse characteristics and ways of life. He has created us members of different
races, each with its own peculiar gifts and endowments.

These differences would seem naturally to justify variety in religious ritual and custom. Some people will prefer simplicity and austerity in worship; others will prefer movement and colour and ceremonial. Some will value the help of music and pictures and flowers and ornaments. Others will care for none of those things. And in the life and worship of the reunited Church there should surely be room for different forms and modes of worship, differences of devotional practice and ceremonial custom. There must, that is to say, be room for freedom as well as for tradition, for diversity within unity. One of the most important questions is as to what minimal uniformity is necessary both as an expression and a safeguard of visible unity. Must there, for example, be uniformity of ministerial order, or in the use of a prayer book? But what is of cardinal importance is that in the end we shall achieve a sufficient degree of unity in doctrine and discipline to enable all to join in prayer as in praise with other Christians, to make possible free exchange of pulpits, and to enable all to sit together at the Lord's Table.

Finally, have we given sufficient weight to the promised presence and guidance of the Holy Spirit in the Church throughout its history? It is true that the manifold sins and weaknesses within the Body of Christ have sorely marred its life, and spoilt its witness. But surely even the sins of schism and division have not altogether frustrated the promised guidance of the Spirit. And wherever the Church as a whole, or any group within it, is truly and humbly seeking that guidance, it will be led to a fuller vision of the truth, and a more perfect understanding of God's will. In problems of faith, and life, and order alike, it is not enough only to look back; we must also look forward, and above all, upward, remembering that the Church's life is lived in two dimensions. It is in that conviction surely, that we must face the great issues of our time, and not least, that urgent call to reunion which is sounding so loudly in our ears today, that we dare no longer disregard it.

Theological thought and historical investigation are immensely important. But they are not enough. I close with some noble words of Dr. T. W. Manson, reminding us of this truth:

"Because the Church is a living organism, we cannot simply go back to New Testament times and say that whatever we find there must be binding forever, and that anything in the Church's life and organisation that cannot be shown to have existed in the Apostolic age, has no right to exist at all . . . The final test in a living Church is not, Did this or that exist in the age of the Apostles? but, Is it here and now accompanied by the signs of the ministry of our Lord, in Galilee and Judea? for there the standard and pattern of the continuing ministry were laid down once and for all. We may go back to the achievements of the Church in the past for inspiration, guidance and encouragement. But to set up the Church of the first, or any other century, as the final court of appeal, while professing Faith in the continuing presence of Christ in His Church, and the continuing guidance of His Spirit, seems to me to savour of inconsistency".[1]

[1] *The Church's Ministry:* T. W. Manson. By kind permission of Hodder and Stoughton, Ltd.

THE CHURCH OF SCOTLAND AND
THE ECUMENICAL MOVEMENT

Presidential Address to the Scottish Theology Society

The Ecumenical Movement since its first deliberate and official initiation in 1927 at Lausanne has been steadily if slowly making an impact upon all the Churches. Some are still so suspicious of it, like the Southern Baptists of America, that they hold themselves sternly aloof. But the fact that some two hundred churches are now associated with the World Council of Churches is so significant and impressive that none can deny either the reality or the widespread influence of this movement towards closer unity or, as some are prepared to describe it, the re-integration of Christendom.

Perhaps hardly less striking and significant is the fact that the Ecumenical Movement, which actually began among the Churches of Western lands, now has many, and some of its most ardent supporters, in Asia, so that it was felt right to hold the last meeting of the World Council in New Delhi.

When that has been said, however, it must also be admitted that there are still serious divergencies of view as to what is the ultimate goal of the Movement; in other words, as to what kind of Unity is to be aimed at, as apparently most consonant with the purpose of Christ for his Church on earth. The Executive of the World Council at a recent meeting were able to agree upon a Statement describing this ultimate goal:

"We believe that the unity which is both God's will and his gift to his Church is being made visible as all in each place who are baptised into Jesus Christ and confess him as Lord and Saviour are brought by the Holy Spirit into one fully committed fellowship, holding the one apostolic faith, preaching the one Gospel, breaking the one bread, joining in common prayer, and having a corporate life reaching out in witness and service to all and who at the same time are united with the whole Christian fellowship in all places and all ages in such wise that ministry and members are accepted by all, and that all can act and speak together as occasion requires for the tasks to which God calls his people." (*The New Delhi Report, The Third Assembly of the World Council of Churches.*)[1]

While it is a noble statement, there will probably be many who find themselves unable to accept it, and some to whom it may appear ambiguous and even self-contradictory. Even the drawing up of such a Statement would nevertheless have doubtless been impossible ten years ago.

Quite clearly (as it seems to me) the Executive of the World Council envisages, as the ultimate aim, on the one hand some form of organic reunion between the Churches in any given particular country or neighbourhood, and on the other hand such agreement on matters of Faith and Order that, as between churches throughout the world, there shall be mutual recognition of Ministries and free inter-Communion of members.

If this is the ideal towards which the Ecumenical Movement is directed, then it seems that certain presuppositions fall to be accepted:

1. That, since Christ desires his Church to be 'one', our present divisions are not only unhappy but sinful; even although in historical origin and in present maintenance they were brought about from high and conscientious motives.

2. That, in the present divided state of the Church, no branch or part of it can claim to possess a full apprehension of truth or a full enjoyment of spiritual fellowship or liturgical and sacramental blessing.

3. That each of the now separated parts or branches of the Church has something precious and distinctive to contribute to others.

4. That therefore no particular branch of the Church can legitimately rest content with its separate life and traditions and ecclesiastical customs, as though they had nothing to learn or to receive from others.

5. Finally, that in any reunited Church, whether in South India or Ceylon or England or Scotland, each uniting church must bring its own distinctive contribution; each however being no less willing to receive than to give.

[1] By kind permission of the World Council of Churches and the S.C.M. Press Ltd.

These would seem to be some of the essential presuppositions underlying any genuine participation in the Ecumenical Movement. They obviously involve penitence, charity, patience, humility, and a readiness for sacrifice—qualities which are not yet perhaps conspicuously evident in any of the Churches, and yet without which little real progress is likely to be seen.

Whatever may be our ultimate conclusion as to the kind of ecclesiastical unity envisaged by the New Testament and desired by him who is the Head of the Church, the Ecumenical Movement has had the salutary effect of compelling us, whether as individuals or denominations, to examine once again the origins, claims and doctrinal basis of that branch of the Church to which we ourselves belong.

How good for us thus to be disturbed out of our ecclesiastical smugness or indifference, to be forced to face difficult and sometimes uncomfortable questions! Those of us who are older and can recollect a time before discussions of reunion became so urgent and so well publicised must admit that we were brought up in a sort of Presbyterian complacency which we accepted with ease!

Moreover, how seldom most of us face the fact that our membership of a particular branch of the Church is almost entirely a matter of family tradition or geographical chance. How few people think of saying, Why am I a Presbyterian, Episcopalian, Congregationalist?

Scottish Church history for the last four hundred years has been distinguished by its astonishing tendency to theological controversy, leading to one division or separation after another. In each case, those who brought about the cleavage or separation were confident that some vital principle of Christian belief or ecclestiastical principle was at stake.

*　　　*　　　*

It has been left to our own time to rediscover another Christian principle, which leads in the opposite direction: namely, towards the unity of the Church. It is rediscovery of this belief which has given birth to the Ecumenical Movement. We have at least begun to ask ourselves whether schism is not frequently a sin; whether some of our continued divisions are not indeed largely due to non-theological causes difficult to justify, and whether Christ is not calling us to take every possible step to break down our denominational barriers.

We in the Church of Scotland, by reason of our religious situation, have been peculiarly prone to fall into complacency: our form of church government guaranteed by Act of Parliament, our large majority of membership affording a sense of security and power.

So that, as I have said, it is undoubtedly good for us to be shaken out of this complacency by the Ecumenical Movement.

When we approach the actual challenge of the breaking down of the barriers which divide different groups of Christians from one another, two different attitudes are possible. One can either say: How far can I defend the ecclesiastical position and traditions to which I belong? or one can say: What contribution can the ecclesiastical doctrine and system to which I belong make to a re-integrated Christendom? And even although the conclusions in either case might conceivably be very similar, the attitudes of mind are quite different, and serve to create an altogether different attitude. The first is defensive; the second is co-operative and creative.

To dig ourselves in, in a kind of Maginot Line of ecclesiastical polity, is untrue to the whole spirit of the Reformation which, in certain of its aspects, was a liberation.

So much by way of general approach towards ecumenical conversation. Where then, do we ourselves, as a Reformed Church, stand? Officially, we are really committed to ecumenical conversation, on certain conditions. To begin with, we can recall the short but very hopeful statement adopted by the General Assembly in 1954:

"The Church of Scotland, believing in one Holy Catholic and Apostolic Church, and acknowledging one Baptism for the remission of sins, affirms its intention of seeking closer relations with every other Church with which it stands in fundamental doctrinal agreement, but from which it is separated in matters of government and the ordering of the ministry.

"In its approach to other Churches in which it discerns the one Body of Christ, the Church of Scotland would desire to look beyond the divisions of history to the ultimate fulness and unity of the Church's life in Christ, and to affirm its readiness to consider how the contributions of all such Churches may be embraced within that unity and fulness; always, however, in agreement with the Word of God and the fundamental doctrines of the Christian faith.

"In such approaches the Church of Scotland would seek to join, humbly and penitently, with its sister Churches in fulfilment of the Lord's prayer that all who believe in Him might be one" (*Reports of the General Assembly*).[1]

So, too, in the *Articles Declaratory of the Constitution of the Church of Scotland in Matters Spiritual*, we read:

"The Church of Scotland, believing it to be the will of Christ that His disciples should be all one in the Father and in Him, that the world may believe that the Father has sent Him, recognises the obligation to seek and promote union with other Churches in which it finds the Word to be purely preached, the sacraments administered according to Christ's ordinance, and discipline rightly exercised; and it has the right to unite with any such Church without loss of its identity on terms which this Church finds to be consistent with these Articles."

It is well to be clear as to what is meant by the name 'Church of Scotland'.

Recently in a joint discussion in which I took part, I heard a clergyman of a different Communion declare that the Church of Scotland traced its origin to the Reformation! This misleading statement is of course ludicrously false. As the *Scots Confession of 1560* puts it:

"As we believe in one God, Father, Son and Holy Ghost, so do we most constantly believe that from the beginning there has been and now is and to the end of the world shall be one Kirk, that is to say one company and multitude of men chosen of God who rightly worship and embrace Him by true faith in Jesus Christ, who is the only head of the same Kirk, which also is the body and spouse of Christ Jesus, which Church is catholic, that is universal, because it contains the elect of all ages, of all realms, nations, and tongues, be they of the Jews, or be they of the Gentiles, which have communion and society with God the Father and with His Son Jesus Christ, through the sanctification of the Holy Spirit; and therefore it is called the com-

[1] By kind permission of the Church of Scotland General Assembly.

munion, not of profane persons, but of saints, who as citizens of
the heavenly Jerusalem have the fruition of the most inestim-
able benefits, to wit, of one God, one Lord Jesus, one faith, and
one baptism: Out of the which Church there is neither life nor
eternal happiness."

The Reformation, that is to say, was not in any sense a break-
away from, but a return to, the beliefs and practices, the order
and worship of the Apostolic Church. Its declared aim was
"to restore the face of the primitive Kirk". What the Reformers
claimed was that the ultimate criterion of both doctrine and
ecclesiastical custom was to be found in the Scriptures of the
Old and New Testaments. All traditions, all Church practices,
all creeds and confessions were to be brought to the one test:
Were they or were they not consonant with the teaching of
Christ, and with the doctrine of the Apostles who had received
both their instructions and their commission from the Master
himself?

The writings of the New Testament were authoritative in a
unique fashion; because they, beyond any other documents or
oral traditions, brought us into touch with the historic Jesus
and risen Lord and those who had been closest to him during
the days of his incarnation. These contentions of course inevitably raise the whole problem of Development, and the authority
of gradually established Tradition. But the only point being made
at this moment is that the Reformers never intended to break
away from, but to return to, the beliefs and ecclesiastical order
and ways of worship of the earliest times. They were convinced
that there is a visible, catholic and apostolic Church on earth
and that the Reformed Churches, whether in Scotland,
England, Switzerland, Holland, Germany, were parts of that
Church.

The central issue in any scheme of reunion between Churches
of different traditions in our own country will vary in different
cases. For example, with the Baptists, the central issue concerns believers' baptism and infant baptism. With Congrega-
tionalists it is that of credal adherence, or conciliar church
government. As between Episcopalian and Presbyterian
churches, the central issue concerns the ministry: its origin, its
nature, its function.

It will be simpler and better if in the rest of this essay I confine myself to the documents of the Reformed Communion with which I am more familiar. To quote therefore the Church of Scotland standards:

"The visible Church which is also catholic and universal under the Gospel, consists of all those throughout the world that profess the true religion, together with their children, and is the Kingdom of the Lord Jesus Christ, the house and family of God out of which there is no ordinary possibility of salvation" (*Westminster Confession of Faith*, Ch. 25: 2).

"Particular visible Churches, members of the general Church, are also held forth in the New Testament. Particular churches in primitive times were made up of visible saints, namely of such as being of age, professed faith in Christ and obedience unto Christ according to the rules of faith and life as taught by Christ and his Apostles, and of their children" (*The Form of Presbyterial Church Government*).

"Unto this catholic visible Church Christ hath given the ministry, oracles and ordinances of God for the gathering and perfecting of the saints in this life to the end of the world, and doth by his own Presence and Spirit, according to his promises, make them effectual thereunto" (*Westminster Confession of Faith*, Ch. 25: 3).

"No man ought to take upon himself the office of a minister of the Gospel until he be lawfully called and ordained thereunto" (*The Form of Church Government Directory for the Ordination of Ministers*).

"It is requisite that ministers be ordained by some who, being set apart themselves for the work of the ministry, have power to join in the setting apart others who are found fit and worthy" (*Ibid.*).

"The offices of the apostles, evangelists and prophets were extraordinary and continued in the Church so long as by the will of God it was needful for the wellbeing of the Church, who although in regard to their order, manner of ministration and the places which they did hold, which is called *Successio in gradum eundem*, they have properly none to succeed them, yet in respect of their doctrine, holiness of life and substance of their ministry which is *successio in caput*, all faithful pastors lawfully called to their functions are their successors" (*The Government and Order of the Church of Scotland in 1641*).

D

From these statements from our own Standards, certain conclusions fall clearly to be drawn.

1. In the belief of the Church of Scotland, the Ministry was given by Christ to the Church and is an essential element in its life and mission.

2. The Ministry has been handed down through the centuries continuously from the Apostles, although this continuity is not regarded as dependent upon actual and mechanically unbroken succession, but upon the grace of God and the intention of the Church.

3. Ordination is to be carried out by prayer and the laying on of hands by those who have themselves been similarly commissioned.

4. Ordination is into the Ministry of the Church Catholic.

5. Ordination is to be carried out, not on the authority of any single congregation, but only on the authority of a duly constituted court. These principles it recognises in the New Testament, and takes therefore as generally normative. As Professor Moffat says:

"Ordination is an act of the presbytery, but in its specific action it is reserved for presbyters who lay hands on the person to be ordained, with prayer. If ordination were merely induction into the order of presbyters, from which some members by a subsequent process were selected to preach, and others to rule, then the service might from its nature belong to all presbyters. But as ordination to the ministry is the solemn consecration of a man to the office of presbyter it is a function which belongs to presbyters as such" (*The Presbyterian Churches*, pp. 115-116).

or, as Lord Balfour of Burleigh puts it:

"It is undoubtedly true that the first generation of Reformed preachers had been nearly all Roman presbyters; that within a few years they began to ordain new presbyters by the laying on of hands; and that there is therefore in the Scottish Presbyterian Churches a *perpetua successio presbyterorum* from before the Reformation" (*Ibid.*, p. 120).

I think our traditional position is well summed up by J. L.

Ainsley in his book, *The Doctrines of Ministerial Order in the Reformed Churches of the Sixteenth and Seventeenth Centuries*:

"We can conclude that Reformed churchmen believed in an unbroken apostolic succession or better still a Christly succession, of the true visible Church, even though they might think that during certain periods that true visible Church had been almost submerged under error. And they were quite convinced that their own Reformed Communions were in the continuity of that 'succession'. In view of this persuasion there is to be noted the care exercised by the Reformed Churches in admission to the ministry. Ministers must be duly commissioned by the true Church. All the arrangements for the admission to the ministry, including the ceremony of ordination, were to insure as far as possible that ministers would have the due authorising of the Church. Of course that did not in the least leave out of account that there must be the authorising of each individual minister by the great Head of the Church, indeed, that went along with the other, in part additionally to it, and in part was carried out by the Church. But the authorising of the Church was there, of that Church which had continued from the Apostles and had all along been authorising ministers of the Church. Consequently all the duly authorised and commissioned ministers were placed in the line of the official ministers which stretched back to the Apostles. Such a 'succession' back to the Apostles, from the very nature of their doctrines both as regards Church and Ministry, the Reformed Church could claim."[1]

While, however, the Church of Scotland regards its own form of ministry, church discipline and government as being consonant with historical doctrine and practice, it does not deny that a similar claim may be made for other forms of church government, such as the Episcopal. It indeed recognises, and is bound to recognise, that in the earliest days ministerial order was tentative and fluid and that even in the second century it developed differently in different localities. Obviously therefore, even the Reformers, eager to refer to the authority of Scripture, could not attempt to reproduce in the sixteenth century the exact form of church order and discipline as those of the first century. Thus Calvin:

[1] By kind permission of T. & T. Clark.

"Since the Lord has not been pleased to prescribe in external discipline and ceremonies every detail which we are bound to follow (foreseeing that this depended upon the nature of the times, and declining to lay down that one form should suit all ages) here we must have recourse to the general rules which He has given, using them to test whatsoever the needs of the Church may require in the interests of order and decorum . . . since matters of this kind are not necessary for salvation and since they ought to be adjusted for the building up of the church in a variety of ways answering the customs of each age and nation, it would be proper to change and abrogate use and wont and also to institute new forms as the interests of the church may require" (*Institutes*, Ch. 4, 1, 30).

If that is so, then obviously we cannot claim that Presbyterian policy is of the *esse* of the Church, as is claimed for Episcopacy by certain Anglican theologians. All that we claim in our standards is that "the Presbyterian government and discipline, as authorised in the church, are founded on and agreeable to the Word of God". So far as the evidence of the New Testament goes, it would surely have to be admitted that Monarchical Episcopacy and the Presbyterian Eldership as we know it today are alike later developments, justified in the experience of the life of the Church.

When therefore we seek to approach this problem of the Ministry in ecumenical conversation, we dare not entrench ourselves dogmatically in our own position, but must allow ourselves to be guided by the general principles of apostolic doctrine and also by the ongoing life of the Church through the centuries.

This raises what I believe, in any Ecumenical conversations between the Reformed Churches and others, is an issue of central importance, and one to which we in Scotland have paid too little attention, the relation of Tradition and Scripture. In an essay such as this there is time to do no more than simply suggest in the briefest manner a certain possible new approach to the problem.

Tradition, as the Protestant Churches have customarily conceived it, has consisted of doctrines and customs, added to the beliefs or practice of some part of the Church, but with no specific authority in Scripture and therefore either to be repudiated or to be regarded with suspicion, as tending to undermine the unique biblical authority. This conception of Scripture and Tradition as possibly opposed to one another is at least implied in the Westminster Confession:

"VI. The whole counsel of God, concerning all things necessary for his own glory, man's salvation, faith and life, is either expressly set down in scripture, or by good and necessary consequence may be deduced from scripture; unto which nothing at any time is to be added, whether by new revelations of the Spirit, or traditions of men. Nevertheless, we acknowledge the inward illumination of the Spirit of God to be necessary for the saving understanding of such things as are revealed in the word; and that there are some circumstances concerning the worship of God, and government of the Church, common to human actions and societies, which are to be ordered by the light of nature and Christian prudence, according to the general rules of the word, which are always to be observed."

This traditional Protestant attitude is, however, based upon a false conception as to the nature of the authority of the Bible, and had the consequence of setting an infallible book over against an infallible Church. Modern biblical scholarship has made such a position no longer tenable. We can no longer think of the whole collection of biblical documents as a once and for all furnished storehouse of doctrines, finding 'proof texts' whether for theological dogmas or ecclesiastical customs. Rather we see them as the record of a continuously developing process of Divine revelation and human response. The Scriptures will always have their unique value, in that they constitute a unique account of that Divine revelation, and in especial because they are for us a unique record of the mighty acts of God, first in his Covenant with his Chosen People, and later in the incarnation, ministry, death and resurrection of his Son Jesus Christ. But this authority, derived from the actual teaching, passion and resurrection of Christ through the Apostles, is utterly different from the authority of an infallible book. As Daniel Jenkins says:

"Protestantism has been disposed wrongly to idealise Scripture. Instead of seeing Scripture as, on one level, part of Tradition, it has been disposed to treat it as a storehouse of ideal

patterns and examples for the moral and spiritual life. Whereas
many of the profoundest lessons of Scripture come home only
to those who understand that it reveals God's dealings with
His people in the uneven, broken contingency of history as it
is lived by sinful men. Thus although they constantly started
from biblical texts, Protestants often succeeded only in taking
the Bible out of history and in gravely falsifying its real message
. . . To regard any suggestion of imperfection in the record, or
confusion in the writer, as a sign of impiety is to break the
fellowship of those who live the common life of the people of
God. It is to imply that the revelation came to men of different
nature from ourselves, who lived in a different kind of world,
and thus that it cannot speak to us where we are" ('Tradition
and the Spirit' in *The Church of God*, edited by E. L. Mascall).[1]

If however we have to revise our conception of the nature
of the Scriptures, it is no less necessary that we should rethink
our conception of the nature of Tradition. The definition of it
offered by the report of the Edinburgh Conference of Faith and
Order seems to suggest a much wider and more satisfying idea:
here it is defined as "the living stream of the Church's life".
Tradition, that is to say, is not a static body of dogmas and
customs handed down from the past, and obligatory simply
because of their antiquity or because of their definition by some
ecclesiastical council or decree. Rather, it is a set of beliefs and
practises developed under the guidance of the Holy Spirit
within the on-going life of the people of God.

Here is surely a conception of Tradition which is consonant
with the promise that the Holy Spirit will lead us into ever new
and fuller insights into God's purposes, and which also makes
possible a more dynamic conception of the whole faith and life
of the Church as a Divinely-sustained organism, living and
growing through the passing centuries.

If we, in the Reformed Churches, are able to accept this
wider and far more fruitful conception of the nature of Tradition, then we shall no longer think of its authority as set over
against the authority of Scripture. We shall still recognise the
uniquely precious and directive value of the Scriptures; but
we shall see them at the same time as in a very real sense part
of Tradition, and indissolubly bound up with it in "the living

[1] By kind permission of the S.P.C.K.

stream of the Church's life". And more than that, we shall realise that, alike in Scripture and in Tradition, the Holy Spirit continues to inspire and guide God's people.

This larger view of Tradition seems to me magnificently expressed in a passage by Father George Florovsky:

"As Khomyakov admirably puts it, 'Neither individuals nor a multitude of individuals within the Church preserve tradition or write the Scripture, but the Spirit of God which lives in the whole body of the Church.' 'Concord with the past' is only the consequence of loyalty to the whole; it is simply the expression of the constancy of catholic experience in the midst of shifting times. To accept and understand tradition we must live within the Church, we must be conscious of the grace-giving presence of the Lord in it. We must feel the breath of the Holy Ghost in it. We may truly say that when we accept tradition we accept, through faith, our Lord, who abides in the midst of the faithful; for the Church is His body, which cannot be separated from Him. That is why loyalty to tradition means not only *concord* with the past, but, in a certain sense, *freedom from* the past, as from some outward formal criterion. Tradition is not only a protective, conservative principle; it is primarily the principle of growth and regeneration. Tradition is not a principle striving to restore the past, using the past as a criterion for the present. Such a conception of tradition is rejected by history itself and by the consciousness of the Church.

"Tradition is *authority to teach, potestas magisterii, authority to bear witness to the truth*. The Church bears witness to the truth not by reminiscence or from the words of others, but from its own living, unceasing experience, from its catholic fulness . . . Tradition is the constant abiding of the Spirit, and not only the memory of words. Tradition is a *charismatic*, not a historical, principle" (G. V. Florovsky, 'Sobornost: the Catholicity of the Church' in *The Church of God: an Anglo-Russian Symposium* edited by E. L. Mascall).[1]

Now the relevance of all this to ecumenical conversation is at once obvious. For if we can escape from the arid conception of an infallible book and from the no less arid conception of Tradition as a fixed body of rigidly defined doctrines and cus-

[1] By kind permission of the S.P.C.K.

toms, then the way is open to ask whether the Holy Spirit in our time is perhaps leading all of us, Christians of various different Communions, to discover some new and still larger insight into God's will for his Church.

It is in the light of this more dynamic conception that I believe we have, as a Reformed Church, to approach the Ecumenical Movement, and prepare both to learn from others and to make our own distinctive contribution.

Finally, it may be asked: What are those distinctive elements in the belief and practice of the Church of Scotland which constitute the chief contribution which we can bring into a re-united Church? I suggest they are at least three:

I. THE BELIEF IN THE SPIRITUAL FREEDOM OF THE CHURCH: its right to order its own worship and polity

It is this conviction which runs through the whole religious history of Scotland. Inevitably it was written into the *Articles Declaratory of the Constitution of the Church of Scotland in Matters Spiritual.*

"This Church, as part of the Universal Church wherein the Lord Jesus Christ has appointed a government in the hands of Church office-bearers, receives from Him, its Divine King and Head, and from Him alone, the right and power subject to no civil authority to legislate, and to adjudicate finally, in all matters of doctrine, worship, government, and discipline in the Church . . ."

In mediaeval times, the power and authority of the Papacy was so great in all European countries that the problem of the spiritual freedom of the Church did not arise. When in Scotland at the Reformation the Papal authority was disowned, the Church had to come to terms with the State. It was not long before the appointment of bishops by the Crown was seen to threaten the liberty of the Church, and the abuse of that right by the King was one reason why in Scotland Episcopacy became suspect and finally detested.

In the Westminster Confession the authority of the Civil Magistrate in his own sphere is fully recognised. But it is also laid down that, so far as moral and ecclesiastical matters are concerned, it is the duty of the Civil Magistrate to support the

Church, and if need be to assist the moral authority of the Church by legal or even police sanctions!

Again and again during the last four hundred years, this assertion of the spiritual freedom of the Church in its worship, creed and polity has been made, often at great cost: in the struggle of the Covenanters against the Divine Right of Kings; against bishops and prayer book imposed by the Crown; in the origin of the Relief Church and the protests of the Seceders; in the fight against patronage; and finally in the dramatic Disruption of 1843 which almost divided in two the whole Christian population of Scotland.

It is out of this struggle for spiritual freedom that there has emerged that settlement of the relationship between Church and State in Scotland, which is the envy of many other countries; a settlement which has given us a Church both national and free. And it is significant that at this very moment a new initiative has been taken south of the border to secure for the Church of England greater influence in the appointment of her own bishops and other church dignitaries. Here is a principle and conviction which we can bring with humble confidence into any ecumenical conversation.

2. The second distinctive element in the Reformed Church heritage would seem to be A BELIEF IN THE IMPORTANCE AND THE AUTHORITY OF THE PULPIT

This needs no elaboration. The Reformers saw that the chief and most urgent remedy alike for the ignorance and the moral laxity of the people was to be found in regular preaching and teaching of Christian doctrine and ethical standards. They made this in Scotland one of their first aims; and although for many decades it was difficult to achieve, owing to the shortage of educated clergy, that aim was never lost sight of. Generation by generation, and still today, the importance of the proclamation of the Word, and the necessity of a theologically educated ministry, have been ideals peculiarly distinctive of Reformed Churches. And the influence of the pulpit in shaping the character and convictions of our own Scottish people can scarcely be exaggerated.

This stress laid on preaching has sometimes been misunderstood. We are accused of attributing an exaggerated importance to the sermon. But our belief in the authority of the pulpit, and that which gives even the youngest minister confidence when he climbs its steps, is that this authority is the authority of Christ, mediated through the Scriptures and Tradition and the on-going life of the Church. Never has the task of preaching been more urgently necessary than in our time. Never perhaps has it been more difficult; partly owing to the unfathomable ignorance of the Bible and Biblical background, partly to the widespread materialistic assumptions of an age dominated by scientific categories, and partly by the variety of schools of theological thought. Yet I believe that the revival of Biblical Theology in our time is doing much to restore the traditional Scottish recognition of the importance of the proclamation of the Word, and also to bring back into the pulpit the proper note of authority.

3. Thirdly, there is THE RECOGNITION OF THE RIGHT AND DUTY
    OF THE LAITY TO SHARE IN THE GOVERNMENT AND DISCI-
    PLINE OF THE CHURCH

The Church does not consist only of the clergy. History, moreover, has shown how grave are the dangers both of Episcopal prelacy and of clerical domination. It is an essential conviction of the Reformed Churches that the lay people, through their properly appointed representatives, have a right to take part in the government and discipline of the Church. (How many of us might become small Popes if not restrained and kept humble in our own parishes by our Kirk Sessions!)

In our own Church the responsibility of the laity is focussed in the office of the Eldership, and in some parishes the Deaconship. It cannot be justifiably maintained that the office of the Eldership as we know it today is to be found in Scripture. But it is an historical development which has proved its value beyond all question through many generations. And although not at present being as fruitfully used as it might, it stands for a principle of cardinal importance, emphasises the 'priesthood of all believers', and holds the only promise for the effective re-evangelisation of our semi-pagan twentieth-century society.

Here, in the strengthened rights and responsibilities of the Christian laity, is surely a vitally important contribution which the Reformed Churches can bring into the Ecumenical Movement.

I finish by returning to that conviction which underlies almost every part of this paper: namely, that ecumenical conversation can only be creative and fruitful if those Churches entering into it do so in the belief that not only have they something valuable to give, but no less something valuable to receive from others.

THINGS NEW AND OLD

"When, therefore, a teacher of the law has become a learner in the kingdom of Heaven, he is like a householder who can produce from his store both the new and the old."

St. Matthew 13: 52

Until quite recently I used to go from time to time when I was in Edinburgh to visit one of my old university teachers. A man of commanding intellectual power and equally impressive personality. During his last years, when he had passed the eightieth milestone of his earthly journey, he was seldom able to travel beyond the boundaries of his own garden; and for the last year, was confined almost completely to bed.

He was a fascinating conversationalist, and every time I saw him I was struck by two things: the immense range of his reading and knowledge of history and of literature of all the centuries, and at the same time his intense interest in the present, the newest developments in the realm of science, the newest work of biography, or latest political event or personal adventure.

If one were asked to define what are the marks of a truly mature and cultured mind, I think one of the chief of such marks would be the ability to appreciate what is best both in the past and in the present; a sensitiveness to the value alike of tradition and of change.

It is not easy to keep that double alertness. Some of us, partly by temperament, partly perhaps due to the particular circumstances and experiences of our own lives, are traditionalists; holding tenaciously to the past, accepting the standards of taste and custom handed down to us by our forebears, moved to admiration and reverence by the appeal of antiquity; determined to walk 'in the old ways'. Others of us, with a different temperament and perhaps different circumstances and experience, are radicals; despising the past, impatiently pushing aside the standards of value once accepted as authoritative, spurning ancient customs, welcoming whatever is new and revolutionary and exciting, deliberately knocking down the old signposts and refusing to walk in the old ways.

Is this then the choice that confronts us: either to join the revolutionists, the angry young men set upon creating a brave new world, or alternatively to associate ourselves with the staid company of the diehards, insensitive to the challenge of change, always looking backwards rather than forwards for inspiration?

Our text suggests a different attitude: "When, therefore, a teacher of the law has become a learner in the kingdom of Heaven, he is like a householder who can produce from his store both the new and the old."

I believe this saying of Jesus our Lord states a truth which is of profound and immense relevance in this contemporary world, and this age of transition through which we are living. It is relevant in many different spheres of life and activity: a reminder of the need for ability to appreciate what is best both in the past and in the present.

We of this exciting tumultuous twentieth century are conscious of this tension between the old and the new in almost the whole field of literature and art. Some of us, for example, in the realm of poetry, dearly love Spenser and Milton, Coleridge and Wordsworth; and in spite of all modern efforts of debunking, shall go on holding to these older loves. But how tragic will be our loss if we refuse to learn the new language and try to enter into the new and fascinating poetic forms of Dylan Thomas or T. S. Eliot or W. H. Auden.

The same is true of architecture. To those of us who love the romantic Gothic beauties of an Oxford college or an ancient cathedral church, it is startling to be confronted for the first time by the skyline of an American city. But after a few weeks in New York, one begins to discover that many of the vast austere skyscrapers have a dignity and elegance of their own, and that there is a certain fascination and functional fitness about even the huge glass matchbox within which the affairs of the United Nations Organisation are carried on!

It is the same in the realms of music, of sculpture, of painting. How insufferably vain and silly would be the person who could not value the great artistic creations of past centuries. But how much we miss also if we do not attempt to learn at least something of the new language in which Henry Moore or Picasso or Debussy is speaking to our own day and generation.

In a slightly different form, we can see this same tension between old and new in the argument carried on, in recent years, in academic circles between the classicists and the scientists. At the moment the battle may be swinging in favour of the scientists, exhilarated by the success of their incredibly daring experiments and researches. But sooner or later the argument will surely reach the solution that a liberal education for Modern Man must be an education which takes into account both the classical heritage of the great ages of the past and the scientific disciplines and achievements of our own time. For the good scholar must be like a "householder who can produce from his store both the new and the old".

This great saying of our Lord is no less true and no less relevant in the realm of religion. For in these words Jesus is thinking of the relationship of his own teaching to the teaching of earlier Judaism. In many ways he was himself a traditionalist. He was steeped in the ancient Hebrew Scriptures. He quotes from the beloved book of Psalms. He doubtless learned by heart, when he was a boy, whole chunks of the books of the Law and of the Prophets. He was regular in attendance at the services of the synagogue. When he went to Jerusalem, he instinctively, like every devout Jew, made his way to the Temple. He dearly loved the long religious heritage into which he had been born.

And yet, at the same time he refused to be fettered by that great tradition. He ruthlessly tears down the barbed-wire fences of petty ecclesiastical and social rules which the Pharisees and Scribes had so carefully erected generation after generation. He brusquely brushes aside even the regulations governing the Sabbath, shocking conventional bystanders by healing a sick man brought to him for help, and condoning the behaviour of his disciples eating ears of grain as they walked through the ripening cornfields. "The Sabbath was made for the sake of man, and not man for the Sabbath."

He does far worse things than that. He makes friends with disreputable people, such as tax-collectors and men and women of bad repute. He refuses to pronounce condemnation on a woman actually caught in an act of adultery. The leaders of conventional society, the leaders of religious respectability, hated him, feared him, eventually seized and killed him as a dangerous revolutionary; because he insisted on propagating new ideas, holding up new standards of behaviour, suggesting a new order of society, offering people new insights into the nature of God and into the meaning of their own lives: "Like a householder who can produce from his store both the new and the old." And before he left this earth, he assured his followers that they should expect this process to go on, that they must keep their minds alert and sensitive; for he would send them his Holy Spirit who would lead them into further truth.

Here then surely is a word of clear direction for the Christian Church: it must show a sensitiveness both to the heritage of the past and the value of Tradition, but no less to the challenge of the present and the need for change, movement and experiment.

We cannot ignore the importance of tradition. Christianity is not a new religion. It traces its ancestry back to the times of the great Hebrew Prophets and the Law once given to the people of Israel. But above all, it traces the source of its power and authority to certain mighty acts of God in history: the incarnation, the earthly life, the death and resurrection of Jesus Christ, Son of Man and Son of God. There, we believe, in that historical Person, God revealed himself, God spoke, God acted, God showed forth his purposes for our world as never before or since.

He it was who founded the Christian Church, with its mission to the whole human race. He it was who gave to the Church his Word and his Sacraments. He it was who appointed its first Ministers. He it was who taught us how best to say our prayers. He it was who gave us the great injunction which sums up all the principles and ideals of the Good Life: "To love God with all our hearts and to love our neighbour as ourselves." And under his continuing guidance, the Church through the centuries has been steadfast in these great beliefs and loyal to those observances; each generation handing down to the next those precious things which must never be lost or surrendered.

That is Tradition. And how vitally important it is both in the history and life of the Church and in the Christian life of each one of us.

Yet no less important is the need for new visions, new insights, new ventures, fresh thinking. A static Church would be a moribund Church. But a Church that believes in the Holy Spirit can never be static. It looks forwards as well as backwards. It is ready for creative experiment. It is open to new knowledge.

Take as illustration the light shed by modern scholarship upon Holy Scripture. For more than 1,500 years Christians have turned for guidance, solace and inspiration to that collection of sacred documents, the Bible. It was recognised, in a very real sense, as being the Word of God. It was believed that from its pages, in unique fashion, God speaks; reveals his purposes, rebukes and challenges and comforts. For many centuries, it is true, few could read this book except priests and clerks. But at the Reformation the Bible began to become a book familiar to ordinary folk. They turned to it for light upon the mysteries of Ultimate Reality, for guidance on all the problems of life. But our forefathers read it without an understanding of its literary or historical background. They did not realise the variety of its contents. They regarded all its documents as of equal spiritual value and moral authority; every page in it too sacrosanct for criticism; every sentence to be accepted without question.

Within the last century modern scholarship has been directed upon the Bible with intense care and concentration. It has helped us to recognise the varied historical circumstances in which its different books were composed. It has helped us to distinguish between history and myth and science. It has shown us the great conception of God and his purposes developing in men's minds through the centuries. In the process, it has undoubtedly shattered certain old assumptions, and dealt a deadly blow to the doctrine of an infallible book!

What is to be our attitude towards this new knowledge of the Bible?

I believe it must be twofold. In the first place, we must hold with complete conviction that the Bible is what countless men and women have found it to be through the centuries: a book from the pages of which God speaks, reveals to us himself and his purposes, rebukes and challenges and comforts. A book that can never be superseded but must occupy a unique place in the life of the Church and of individual Christians.

But at the same time we must not be afraid of the remarkable researches and discoveries of modern scholarship but welcome them as helping us to a fuller and more intelligent understanding of the most precious and fascinating collection of writings in the world. The opponents of this new knowledge of the Bible are in reality not helping but hindering the cause of

Christianity, in an age when science is rightly underlining the importance of intellectual integrity. Advances in knowledge can never bring discredit upon any true revelation of God. For "a teacher of the law has become a learner in the kingdom of Heaven, he is like a householder who can produce from his store both the new and the old."

A Church that believes in the Holy Spirit can never be static. It will look forwards as well as backwards. Never has it been more important than it is at this particular hour in history for the Church to be alert to the new situations and problems and needs of the contemporary world. We who are Christians must keep our minds and hearts constantly open to new ways along which the Holy Spirit may be seeking to lead us. We must welcome new knowledge. We must be ready for creative experiment. In the light of rapidly changing conditions of social life, the Church must think out new methods of getting its Gospel across to the man-in-the-street who is often reluctant to listen. We ministers must not be afraid to devise new patterns of worship for men and women who are inclined to feel that all worship is dull or irrelevant. All of us who have heard and accepted the call of Christ to obedience and service must discover new forms of Christian witness in our various trades and professions and fields of daily work.

Only in so far as the Church is both loyal to "the faith once delivered to the saints"; and at the same time sensitive to the spirit of the age, and the urgent new problems and movements of our time, will its voice be listened to and its influence be felt.

E

THEOLOGY AND THE LAYMAN

"Love the Lord your God . . . with all your mind."

St. Luke 10: 27

Many people appear to imagine that religion is concerned chiefly with pious emotions or devotional observances or charitable actions. Jesus reminds us in this saying that religion involves not only the feelings and the will, but also the mind.

Not long ago a Church of England scholar produced a book *Honest to God* which turned out to be a theological best-seller, and is still being talked about in all sorts of unexpected quarters. I think I bought my own copy on a railway bookstall! This is, to most of us, an altogether surprising phenomenon. Because the general assumption is that theology is the concern of the scholar in his study or the preacher in his pulpit; that it is a specialised field of thought in which only the few are interested and in which only a few obtain proficiency. Perhaps the existence of a Faculty of Divinity in the universities serves to encourage this idea; and undoubtedly systematic theology, understood in a technical sense, is a specialised study. I would like, however, to suggest that in the broader sense of the word—namely as thinking about God and His purposes and the meaning of human existence—theology ought to be the concern of Everyman.

Jesus said: "Love the Lord your God . . . with all your mind."

Certainly St. Paul takes this for granted. In his Letters, written to congregations consisting almost entirely of simple and comparatively uneducated people he asks his hearers, without any sort of apology, to follow him in most profound thinking about the greatest subjects. Read, for example, the first section of his Letters to the Colossians. We find the same kind of thing in the fourth century, when disputation was going on about the relationship within the Blessed Trinity between God the Father and Christ the Son. Gregory of Nyssa amusingly refers to this: "Constantinople is full of mechanics and slaves who are all of them profound theologians. If you desire a man to change a piece of silver, he informs you wherein the Son differs from the Father. If you ask the price of a loaf, you are told by way of reply that the Son is inferior to the Father. And if you enquire whether your bath is ready, the answer is that the Son was made out of nothing."

In older days in Scotland, one finds again something of this widespread interest in great religious questions, and one need only open the Shorter Catechism in order to realise the strenuous demands made on the intelligence even of children. For example, the question, "What is God?" Answer: "God is a Spirit, infinite, eternal and unchangeable in His wisdom, being, power, holiness, justness, goodness and truth. There are three Persons in the Godhead: the Father, the Son, and the Holy Ghost, and these three are One God, the same in substance, equal in power and glory." This was learnt by boys and girls of ten years old!

One of the most reassuring signs of the present age is that there appears to be a growing interest in what the Christian Faith has to say about God, about the world, and about man's place in the universe, about the problem of evil and the mystery of suffering. Yet many people, and perhaps especially those of the younger generation, are not satisfied with time-honoured answers given in time-honoured terminology. The answers, it is felt, must be relevant to the needs and problems of the new age in which we are living, and in harmony with the new advances in knowledge. As the Dean of Harvard Divinity School, Dr. Samuel H. Miller, said recently in a striking Address, "Answers cribbed from the back of a book will not suffice to meet the problems now raised by more complicated factors of contemporary culture. The ancient dogmas no longer dominate the imagination. The modern divisions no longer capture men's loyalties. The shape of life has changed; the patterns of truth are different; the questions have new terms; doubts have deeper dimensions. We need the warning of Herman Melville, 'Woe to him who seeks to pour oil upon the waters when God has brewed them into a gale'."

What, then, of the dangers of heresy, of false beliefs? We cannot expect altogether to avoid that risk. Indeed, the Church owes a certain debt to the heretics, if only because constantly through the centuries they prevented the Church falling theologically asleep. A Church without rebels might well become moribund. For conservatism is one of the constant temptations of any great and ancient institution. To return to the book already referred to: in some quarters there has been an outcry against the Bishop of Woolwich for challenging many traditional assumptions and propounding dangerous new doctrines. Undoubtedly there are statements and arguments in his book with which some of us would violently disagree. But whether we agree with his views or not, let us recognise that he has done a real service to theology, in compelling us to think furiously about some of the greatest of all questions. His book has had a far larger sale than most novels, and his unorthodox opinions have at least made religion a vital talking point in many quarters where it is usually ignored. In other words, he has challenged us to try to love God with all our minds. What is primarily important is not whether we find it easier to talk of a "God up there" or a "God out there" or "God within"; but that we should turn our attention to God. And don't let us be afraid of thinking that may perhaps lead to apparently disturbing or even shocking conclusions. It may finally lead to new discoveries of truth.

Another fact must be recognised. The heretics have often proclaimed some aspect of religious truth which has been ignored or forgotten. They perhaps see things out of perspective, but their exaggerated emphasis may itself be valuable. For example, it may be good for a rigid Calvinist preacher, passionately proclaiming the doctrine of predestination, to have a Palagian critic at hand to give an occasional tug to his Geneva gown!

More than that, sometimes the heretics have been in the right. For example, orthodox theology under the influence of Greek philosophy has for centuries proclaimed that God is incapable of suffering, for that would imply a flaw in his perfection. There came the World War with all its horrors, the wounding and death of tens of thousands of young men, and, in the midst of the horror and suffering, an Irish Army Chaplain, Studdart Kennedy, who fearlessly challenged that orthodox belief. Today few, even among theologians, would be prepared to reject the idea of a God who suffers, or to deny that his love for us men with all our blunders, blindness and wickedness inevitably involves, for a God of love, pain and anguish.

Yes, sometimes the heretics have been right. And if there is any moral in that fact, it is surely this, that we Christians should continually be trying to apply our minds to a better understanding of the great truths of the Christian Faith, testing them out in the harsh crucibles of human experience and against the stark facts of history. We are living in a new and exciting era. And if we indeed believe in the Holy Spirit, then we must surely believe that he may at any time have new aspects of truth to show us; aided, it may be, by new discoveries in the realm of science or of biblical scholarship, or by our own reason applying itself to great themes. This openness of mind and intellectual alertness is specially called for at this moment. As is said in a recent statement by a group of Quaker thinkers: "The last word has never yet been spoken on the implications of Christianity, and every religious expression is open to critical examination. We believe, therefore, that it is right for a Christian to ask every kind of question fearlessly in search for truth." "The qualities mainly called for today," says Dr. A. R. Vidler, "are openness to the future, a willingness to travel light or in the dark, patience and imagination in experiment, a large toleration of variety and diversity, based not on indifference but on trust, in the continued guidance of the Holy Spirit."

This is not to advocate a kind of genial and continuing agnosticism. Far from it. We who are convinced Christians hold certain great beliefs, which we believe provide a clue to the very meaning of the universe and the meaning of our own lives. These beliefs are the Christian Gospel. It is a tremendous creed: the belief that this universe is the work of a Creator of infinite power; that at a certain moment in time there was born on this earth a unique man; a man who shared our human life in all its heights and depths; a man who, because of his loyalty to truth and irrepressible moral courage, was ruthlessly done to death on a cross; but who came back from death, back from the tomb, and is alive. A man who was none other than the Son of God himself, rescuing the human race from sin and despair, and by his death and resurrection opening before us eternal horizons.

But perhaps you say, I must have some proof, some kind of demonstration, before I can believe. There is no proof. We recognise today that the old philosophical arguments attempting logically to demonstrate God's existence are in fact no proofs. God can only be apprehended by faith. And faith is a venture, a 'calculated risk' if you like. Some people have the courage to make that venture; others refuse. Yet there is value in the very making of the venture, in the taking of the risk. As a modern thinker has said, "God has refused to give me certainty about himself because certainty leads to false security. Faith gives to life those necessary qualities of mystery and adventure which certainly would kill. Faith enables men to grow in character and to develop in spiritual stature. Faith calls out the best in man, and at the same time leads him to put his reliance not on himself but on God."

It is in that spirit that we accept the great Christian beliefs. Accept them, because they seem, better than any other philosophy or creed, to fit the facts, to explain to us the nature of the universe and the meaning of life. Accept them, because we believe they have been 'revealed', given to us by God himself. Accept them, because they are rooted in history, and have been verified in human experience. Accept them, because they speak to something in the depth of our own being so that we say 'Yes' to them not only with our minds but with our hearts.

Some of those reading this may be saying: That is all very well, as pulpit talk, but what of the contradictions and inconsistencies between theology and science? It has frequently been assumed that science and religion are in conflict. Religious thinkers have been suspicious of scientific research and its conclusions. Scientists for their part have been contemptuous of theological dogmatism. As a result, there has too often been a separation, or at least a lack of conversation and mutual interest, which has meant impoverishment on both sides.

The curious illusion persists that somehow science and religion are rivals, based on incompatible assumptions and inconsistent views of the universe, and that one has to choose whether to associate oneself with those in one camp or the other. There are of course notable exceptions, but roughly speaking, that is the common view. I want to suggest that that assumption is not only unjustifiable but that it is doing grave harm, both to religion and to science.

Actually, science and theology have much in common. For both are concerned with an investigation into the nature of Reality, and of man's place and powers and opportunities within the total structure of Reality. It is sometimes suggested that science deals with facts, and religion with values. But even that is not quite accurate, because both alike recognise the supreme value, Truth. The pursuit of Truth, the apprehension of Truth, in however fleeting glimpses or fragmentary forms, an open-minded readiness to recognise and accept any discovered aspect of Truth, however strange and unexpected— these ideals are common and essential alike in the fields of science and religion.

I would suggest further that there are two qualities which are essential alike to the scientist in his laboratory, the theologian in his study or the religious man on his knees; I mean wonder and humility. Without wonder and humility one is not likely to achieve any true understanding of Reality. Wonder at the inexhaustible, unfathomable richness and variety and complexity of the universe and of human personality. Humility as one realises the limitations of the human mind and the pettinesses and perversions of the human heart when faced by the grandeur of Reality. Moreover, the greater the advances in knowledge, the stronger becomes the call to wonder and humility. And it is significant that it is those who see deepest into the mystery of Reality, the great scientist or philosopher or poet or artist or saint, who show most strikingly these qualities of humility and wonder.

It is of course true that science and religion have different starting points, employ different language, work with different concepts and equipment. But the interpretations of Reality which they offer are not contradictory but complementary. Here is the tribute of a great contemporary scientist, a physicist, speaking of his own profession:

"Our scientific vocation cannot be the whole of life, for it cannot satisfy all our needs. We must not forget that there are other values and other experiences . . . there are the ways of thought which do not change, whose concern is with the things that will not be superseded. And today we stand in need of these sustaining and enduring values of the spirit, more than ever," says Sir Edward Appleton.

I believe that the greatest forward movement for mankind in our time will become possible only if science and religion, yes, and art and poetry, see themselves to be not rivals but partners. More than that, I believe that the moment for such a coming closer in respect and understanding is ripe—if only we are brave enough and open-minded enough to seize it. And here perhaps in especial is one of the great tasks of those who enjoy a university education: the task of glimpsing a synthesis of the different aspects of human knowledge and experience which will give us a fuller and more splendid conception of Reality and of human life than any yet achieved.

Which brings me to the last thing I would like to say. We have been thinking about faith in God. But faith in God is never a purely intellectual activity. It involves the emotions and the will as well as the mind. Jesus said, "You are to love God with all your heart, and with all your mind and with all your strength." That means not only belief in God but trust in God. Not only trust, but also obedience; obedience in the practical decisions, the personal relationships, the tensions and testings and struggles, of everyday life in the world.

II. THE CHURCH AND THE WORLD

SCIENCE AND RELIGION

A sermon preached before the British Association for the Advancement of Science.

"In the beginning God created the heaven and the earth."
Genesis 1 : 1

"For God is love; and his love was disclosed to us in this, that he sent his only Son into the world to bring us life."
1 John 4: 9

"In the beginning God created the heaven and the earth." I have deliberately chosen as our text this quotation from the first chapter of Genesis, because almost a hundred years ago it constituted one of the chief battlegrounds in what many believed to be a life-and-death conflict between science and religion. One of the fiercest engagements in that ideological war was started by the publication of Charles Darwin's famous book, *The Origin of Species*. The views which he then put forward appeared to strike at the very fundamental Christian doctrines both of God and of man. They seemed, moreover, to cast a blight upon the whole authority of Holy Scripture as the Word of God. Either the theories of Charles Darwin, or the great ancient Christian belief about the Creation, must be rejected. Either the biologists were dangerous heretics or the Christian believers were credulous reactionaries. And on either side, it was plain, something of immense value was at stake. For it would be tragic if the authority of Christian Tradition and Scripture were to be overturned; but no less tragic would it be were the freedom and integrity of scientific research to be denied.

Since that time, two movements have taken place which have completely changed the intellectual climate:

1. The first is the new view of the Bible, given to us as the result of the labours of modern scholarship. For while today the Church still holds as strongly as ever its belief in the authority of the Bible as "the supreme rule of faith and life", it no longer regards that authority as involving the verbal inspira-

tion of all the biblical documents. It recognises indeed that these documents vary greatly alike in historical and in spiritual value, and that they are inevitably coloured and shaped by the social and intellectual conditions of the various periods in which they were written. Above all, it has come to be recognised that the unique value and inspiration of the Bible are not dependent upon its verbal infallibility, but upon its power to communicate to men the reality of God, his nature and his purposes.

2. The other significant fact that has helped to transform the intellectual climate is the new attitude of the scientist. For some considerable time it seemed that the acid of scepticism was steadily eating away the traditional Christian doctrines and that the crude creed of materialism had displaced belief in God. That crude creed of materialism has, however, itself become obsolete, submerged under the advancing tide of wider scientific knowledge. Moreover, as was pointed out by B. H. Streeter:

"The very meaning of the words Time, Space, Matter, Energy, Mechanism and Law, as used in modern physics, has become quite different from the meaning of those words in everyday life. And the meaning is different because the concepts to be expressed are not really capable of being expressed in words at all, but only in complex and abstract mathematical symbols."

At the same time many leading scientists today are ready to acknowledge that they are concerned with only one aspect of the universe, and that other aspects no less important must be recognised. Few would now maintain that science is the only valid instrument of knowledge. In other words, today, both theologian and scientist realise that, in their approach to truth and reality, two qualities are above all essential: reverence and humility. Reverence, because that which we do know is so inexpressibly marvellous and beyond all former dreams of the human imagination; humility, because there are so many things that we do not know, mysteries that seem to transcend the range of human reason. Here, for example, are some words written by one of the most distinguished of contemporary scientists, Einstein:

"The most beautiful and most profound emotion we can experience is the sensation of the mystical. It is the sower of all true science. He to whom this emotion is a stranger, who can no longer wonder and stand rapt in awe, is as good as dead. To know that what is impenetrable to us really exists, manifesting itself as the highest form of wisdom and the most radiant beauty which our dull faculties can comprehend only in their most primitive form—this knowledge, this feeling, is at the centre of all true religiousness."

Or here is the personal conviction of a great Scottish teacher, lately Professor of Natural History in the University of Aberdeen. At the conclusion of his Gifford Lectures, Professor J. Arthur Thomson writes:

"We cannot worship Nature. We cannot find abiding human satisfaction in Nature's voices alone. Invigorating, inspiring, and instructive they certainly are, but they are full of perplexities, and it is with a sad wistfulness that we hear their echoes dying away in the quietness of our minds like the calls of curlews on the moor as they pass further into the mist. Happy, then, are those who have what Sir Thomas Browne called 'A glimpse of incomprehensibles, and thoughts of things that thoughts but tenderly touch'. Shall we not seek to worship Him whom Nature increasingly reveals, from whom all comes and by whom all lives."[1]

For too long in popular thought, and perhaps especially among younger people, it has been assumed that it is necessary to choose between a scientific and a religious view of the universe, and that the two are incompatible and mutually exclusive. A man said to me one day recently, "I don't read the Bible, that is old-fashioned stuff. I read the scientific journals." Too often in the past the disciplines of science and theology have been deliberately kept apart. This has resulted not only in misunderstanding, but in serious impoverishment on both sides. What is required now, and what perhaps this second half of the twentieth century is peculiarly well equipped to achieve, is a larger and richer conception of Reality. A conception to which the knowledge of the scientist, the insight of the Christian believer, the vision of the artist and the musician, must alike contribute. For Reality has many facets, and must be seen

[1] *The System of Animate Nature.* By kind permission of Ernest Benn Ltd. for Williams and Norgate.

from many angles before it is fully and truly seen. In the recent Geophysical Year, men of many different nations and lands, of widely different training and background, co-operated in order to secure a true picture of the vast Antarctic subcontinent. So in the great perennial study of the universe, alongside the astronomer and the physicist, the biologist and the historian, there must stand the philosopher, the poet, the mystic and the theologian.

Science and theology are in fact not in opposition, but complementary one to the other; not rivals but partners, alike dedicated to the pursuit of Truth. Rightly understood, the discoveries of science do but illuminate and confirm the beliefs of Christian thinkers. The telescope and the microscope are not the enemies of a religious view of the universe; on the contrary, they reveal to us a universe infinitely more marvellous than our forebears dreamed, and seem to make it more than ever certain that behind all this vast, visible, tangible structure that we call Nature there must be an Infinite Mind and Will: "The heavens declare the glory of God and the firmament showeth his handiwork."

> *Flower in the crannied wall*
> *I pluck you out of the crannie,*
> *I hold you here, root and all, in my hand,*
> *Little flower—but if I could understand*
> *What you are, root and all, and all in all,*
> *I should know what God and man is.*

If it is true that religion benefits by the astonishing advance of science, no less is it true that science needs the inspirations and revelations of religion. For however far scientific knowledge advances, however spectacular its discoveries, it can never give a complete picture of the universe. It can give accurate descriptions, but it cannot make judgments. It cannot attempt to say whether a particular sequence of historical events is good or bad, whether a particular set of actions is right or wrong. The scientist, *qua* scientist, is not even concerned as to whether or not an object is beautiful or ugly. It exists, and he describes it. It happens, and he records it. Yet, as has been well said:

"Science regarded as a quest for Truth cannot ultimately ignore the values which support it or the metaphysical prob-

lems which open up in front of it . . . Science ultimately leads
to the great questions about existence."

Questions which science by itself can never answer, nor indeed
attempt to answer: What is the origin of this mysterious
Universe? What is the meaning of the strange, tumultuous
course of history? What is the purpose and goal of the amazing
process of Life as we see it through its age-long developments and
changes? Or is there any meaning and purpose? Is the universe
friendly or indifferent, co-operative or hostile to us men and
women who have to live in it and who long to understand it?

These are questions which arise naturally in the mind of
any intelligent man: vital, ultimate questions. Where, if anywhere, can we find an answer to them? Surely only through
religion. "In the beginning, God . . ." Only by listening for
a Voice that speaks to us from beyond the boundaries of the
universe. When we open the Bible, we hear that Voice. When
we kneel in prayer, we hear that Voice. Sometimes when we
stand in meditation alone under the open sky, or in a forest
glade or amid the rolling waters of the ocean, in the depths of
our own souls we hear that Voice. Above all when we stand
face to face with a Person, Jesus Christ, and listen to his words
and see him hanging on his Cross, and meet him in the splendour of Easter morning, we hear that Voice. And it answers
the ultimate questions which science cannot answer. Then, and
only then, we know the origin and the meaning and the destiny
of this marvellous universe and of our own human lives set
within it. For the Christian Gospel speaks to us of God: God
the Creator, God the Deliverer, God the sustaining Spirit, God
the Eternal King.

There are in fact two different kinds of knowledge. There is
the knowledge that comes to us through reason, through human
research and discovery; and on the other hand there is the
knowledge that comes to us through what we call 'revelation'.
On the one side the knowledge that has to be striven and worked
for, and on the other side the knowledge that is given. And I
venture to say that there can be no true and complete picture
of the universe, and especially of man's place in it, unless
science is supplemented and transfigured by religion.

"His love was disclosed to us in this, that he sent his only
Son into the world."

We Christians believe that God has once and for all supremely disclosed to us men his nature and purpose, in a human life. A life lived in the midst of history in the little land of Galilee. A life simply and utterly unpretentious in its outward setting, but stamped with a Divine perfection never seen before or since. In the life and character, the death and resurrection of Jesus Christ, God has revealed Himself and His purposes, has shown us the pattern for human life and the essential nature of the universe itself. For in Christ, we believe, is to be found the ultimate key to this vast universe which is our home, and of the whole age-long process of history. In Christ we see focussed, and expressing itself in action, the almighty and all-wise Love which sustains and controls all things visible and invisible. A Love revealing itself not only in creation but in redemption. A Love which ultimately will overcome all that at present seems to us mean, and cruel, and meaningless.

To some people this doctrine of special revelation is difficult, partly because it is unprovable. Yet acceptance of the Christian Gospel does not mean the suspending of reason, still less the surrender of reason. It does mean taking a leap beyond the realm of human reason; what the theologians call "an act of faith". That is not easy. It demands courage. It demands humility. But without such an act of faith, belief is impossible.

To believe that God is Love, that God so loves the world that at a certain moment in history he sent his Son into this world—here is a belief which we must either reject because we cannot prove it, or else accept by an act of humble and courageous faith.

For the man who feels able to accept this Christian Gospel, life takes on a new sense of security and peace, and the whole course of history is flooded with new light and meaning. It is a splendid thing to believe in God the great Creator, Divine Architect of the Universe, Source of Wisdom and Power. It is an even more wonderful thing to believe in God the Great Father whose providence is ever about all his creatures and whose redemptive love seeks us men and women untiringly, one by one. Sooner or later we all come up against experiences that are too much for us—sorrow, suffering, temptation, disappointment, illness, death. Sooner or later we most of us become aware of our own frailty and moral weakness. And at such times we need beliefs about the ultimate realities to sustain us. The man who can say, "I believe in God the Father Almighty . . . I believe in Jesus Christ as Lord and Saviour . . . I believe in the guidance and help of the Holy Spirit . . . I believe in the providential care of God round me even in days of darkness and grief . . . I believe in a life beyond death and the grave"—the man who holds such convictions in his heart has his feet upon a rock, and the wildest storms of life will not be able to move him.

And to those who have not been able to accept such convictions, to those who have not yet found light upon the ultimate mysteries of existence, I would venture to recall words spoken by the supreme Master of Life:

"Seek, and you will find. Knock, and the door will be opened."

THE CHURCH AND THE ARTS
IN SCOTLAND

Presidential Address to the Scottish Ecclesiological Society.

During some three hundred years, the Scottish Church showed singularly little interest in the arts. Sometimes it frowned upon them openly. Sometimes it was content to avert its gaze. And the arts and artists, for their part, as a result, went their own independent way.

There are of course historical reasons to explain this tragic divorce between art and the Church. In the corrupt and ignorant mediaeval Church, meretricious ornament, gaudiness and vulgarity were common; as they are still today in some continental churches. Moreover, teaching given about the Sacraments and about devotional practices in worship were often crude. Add to this the fact that frequently poor folk were taxed and mulcted beyond all bounds to provide unnecessarily luxurious ornaments for the local parish church or, still worse, the distant cathedral.

As a result, the Reformation, when it came to Scotland, swept away not only many obvious and flagrant evils from church life and practice, but also, with those evils, much that was good; and, among other things, all the traditional furnishings and ornaments that once decorated church buildings. In Glasgow Cathedral, for example, where once there were more than thirty altars, the remains of only two can now be seen. All pictures, images, sacred vessels, furnishings, were destroyed. Today in the whole of Scotland only one or two fragments of the lovely mediaeval stained glass remain.

In many cases, even the beautiful buildings themselves were reduced to ruin. Dunblane, Dunkeld, Brechin, Haddington, stood roofless for three hundred years; while Elgin, St. Andrews, and almost all the great abbeys—Melrose, Dryburgh, Jedburgh —are scarcely more than empty shells, only revealing lovely glimpses of their former glory.

The ruthless destruction of the sixteenth century was fol-

F

lowed by the religious quarrels of the seventeenth, and the arid spiritual blight of the eighteenth. During all that time, and almost up to the end of last century, it seemed almost as though the Scottish Church deliberately banished beauty from its sanctuaries. All decoration was suspect. Flowers, pictures, crosses were rejected. The furnishings were of the plainest. Ritual and ceremonial were reduced to the minimum. Even instrumental music was forbidden. Liturgical prayers were frowned upon. No wonder the arts felt as though cold-shouldered by the Church. Whereas, in olden time, craftsmen in wood, in wrought iron, in silver and bronze, in painting and embroidery and stained glass, had done their finest work under the inspiration of religion and in the service of the Church, now artists and craftsmen in Scotland had to dedicate their talents to purely secular purposes. Thus, for more than three hundred years, there stood a great gulf between religion and the arts in Scotland.

It is really only within the last fifty years that a change has gradually begun to take place. Beauty is coming back into the Church. It is inevitably a gradual process, but year by year more people are coming to realise that the House of God is worthy of the best and the loveliest that the imagination of men can conceive and their hands execute. Religion and art belong together. They are not enemies, but allies. Worship is not corrupted or cheapened, but enriched by the aid of colour, light, music, flowers.

But in this revival there lies the danger that we come to forget that, when used in church, art must always be a means and never an end in itself. For example, art in the home and art in the church have quite different functions and its use is inspired by quite different motives. It is sometimes argued, "You like to see your drawing-room looking beautiful with flowers and tapestry and rich rugs. Why not therefore try to make the church equally beautiful so that it is a pleasure to go into it?" A plausible but absolutely false argument. Because one decorates and furnishes one's drawing-room to please oneself and one's friends. But one decorates and furnishes a church to please God and to honour him. Both are justified, but the motives are different. Unless that very elementary and yet enormous distinction is recognised and kept in mind, one can be led into all kinds of mistakes.

Or, to take a different illustration: a priest celebrating the Eucharist wears a magnificent chasuble embroidered and gilded, in honour of the Sacramental rite at which he is officiating. A young man about town wears an embroidered waistcoat to please his own vanity. I remember once a rather dilletante and artistic priest taking me into his sacristy, and showing me an impressive collection of rich and sumptuous vestments for different church festivals and occasions. I was a very young parson, and though impressed, was at the same time rather shocked, without quite knowing why. I know now. I was rightly shocked, because that priest had allowed art to become an end in itself, whereas in the liturgical realm, art must always be only the humble handmaid of religion.

For that reason, it is immensely important for those of us who are concerned with the decoration and beautifying of churches or with the ordering of the ceremonial carried out in them, to be sure that we are guided by the proper principles.

Every ornament or piece of furniture placed in a church should have its place there only for two reasons: either because by its sheer beauty or magnificence it witnesses to and proclaims the glory of God, or else because it serves for the spiritual edification of the worshippers. These are the two fundamental principles which should inspire and guide those who are concerned with the architecture, the decoration and the furnishing of any place of worship: whether it be a large cathedral or a simple small parish church. If these principles are remembered and observed, then fewer mistakes would be made in well-meant schemes of 'restoration' and 'improvement'.

This principle holds along the whole range of church furnishings and ornaments. They are not to be placed there simply because they please the eye. For that, you go to a museum or art gallery. Only that which is erected to glorify God or spiritually edify the worshippers ought to have a place in a sanctuary. When we take care to apply this principle, it gives us valuable guidance in all our ecclesiastical thinking and planning.

If the ornaments and furnishings of a church are to proclaim the glory of God, the Source of all beauty, then they must be the best procurable. Even if it is to be a gift, do not let us accept anything third- or fourth-rate in the way of design or craftsmanship. Better do without than have God's House furnished with what is cheap or inferior.

If a personal illustration may be permitted: many years ago during my first Ministry, one of my parishioners asked if he might present a new Communion Table, which was greatly needed. When I expressed gratitude and appreciation, he then handed me a catalogue of ready-made church furniture and showed me an illustration of a Holy Table, a Minister's Seat, and two other chairs; and said that these were to be his gift. The designs were poor and general appearance of the furniture obviously mediocre in quality. I explained to him, as politely as possible, that I could not accept furnishings of that sort for the church; and suggested that instead we should ask an architect of high standing to prepare a design and instruct a good Scottish firm to make the furniture; that it would be better that he should only give the Holy Table, but have it as fine as possible. It was very difficult at first to persuade him, good Scotsman as he was, to agree to give only one thing when he could have had four things for the same amount of money, and at first he was extremely angry! In the end, however, he agreed; we had a Holy Table simple but strong and beautiful in design and construction, and on the day when it was dedicated he was proud and contented and happy.

Think of this principle as it applies in the sphere of stained glass windows.

At present throughout the whole country there is what almost amounts to a craze for erecting stained glass in churches of every kind, large or small, town or country. The reason is very often simply that it is the fashionable form of ecclesiastical decoration. Just as many people long to instal a modern grate in their living-room because all their acquaintances possess such a grate, so many Kirk Sessions and congregations wish to instal a stained-glass window because they feel it is the correct and fashionable thing to do!

Now there are, as we have seen, really only two good reasons for erecting stained glass in a church. The first is that it is installed as a thing of beauty in homage to God. Unless that is the motive, and unless therefore it can be of the finest quality, there is no good reason for coveting it. This craze has encouraged a large number of commercial firms and a good many rather inferior artists and craftsmen to produce windows which had much better never have been produced! Poor or mediocre quality of design and craftsmanship are seldom either aesthetically or spiritually uplifting, and certainly do not show forth the glory of God, the Supreme Creator of Beauty. Doubtless we have all seen many windows which have injured rather than enhanced the atmosphere of a church. Where the best stained glass cannot be obtained or afforded, it is usually better to have none. This is certainly true of almost all country churches. Why erect some inferior coloured window, often crude and uninspired, when instead it would be possible for the worshipping congregation to see through clear glass the loveliness of hills and sky and trees. When the famous Japanese evangelist, Toyohiko Kagawa, was in this country a few years ago and was being shown round a certain church, he was asked, "Are your own churches in Japan similar to ours?" "Yes," he replied, "except that we do not have these coloured windows. We have plain glass, so that when the congregation cannot understand what is being said from the pulpit, they can look out and understand what God the great Creator is saying and doing in his universe."

Apart from their intrinsic beauty which glorifies God, the other valid reason for installing stained glass in a church is that they are a genuine aid to worship and to an understanding of the Gospel.

In mediaeval times when few people could read and when there was very little preaching in most parishes, partly perhaps owing to the idleness of the priest, partly to the apathy of the average congregation, stained glass, if wisely used, could proclaim the Gospel story in moving and simple fashion. Worshippers could be thus continually reminded, through the eye, of the great central redemptive acts of the Divine drama; the nativity, the crucifixion, the resurrection and the ascension. The parables of our Lord could be vividly illustrated. Or a series of windows could show scenes in the life of the patron saint of the Church. The devotional and educational value of such a use of stained glass is obvious. And I suppose most of us have seen windows of deeply moving spiritual quality. There is one church in central London where I like to say a prayer if possible, partly for the inspiration of kneeling for a moment below a splendid representation of the Saviour on his Cross.

A great many of the fifteenth-century country parish churches in Denmark have the whole Bible story from the Creation to the Last Judgment illustrated by frescoes on the walls and by stained glass in the windows.

So in St. Machar's Cathedral, Aberdeen, in the very fine east window by William Wilson you have set forth in rich and glowing colour the nativity, the crucifixion, and resurrection of our Lord, and the Sacraments of the Church. A window which even if the worshipper's attention were to wander from the sermon (as it would certainly not do if the Minister himself were preaching) would speak to him of the great central mysteries of the Faith. So in our cathedral in Glasgow we have the subjects depicted in the four lights at the centre of the east wall of the quire, the birth, crucifixion, resurrection and ascension, in order that they may form a focus for the eye of all those in that part of the church during Divine Service, and constitute an aid to reverence.

May I give another domestic illustration which shows, in quite a different fashion and from a rather different angle, the importance of keeping the theological motive supreme in the adornment of a church. Not very long ago it was decided to re-glaze the great west window in our cathedral in Glasgow, the theme selected being that of the Creation. Several artists were invited to submit designs. I remember one in particular. It was by a distinguished stained-glass artist; it was extremely pleasing in general effect; the colouring was rich and splendid. But when I looked at it I realised that it was utterly unworthy of its great theme, that it entirely failed to express the majesty of God the Creator of the universe and that therefore, however good artistically, it must be rejected because it was not good enough theologically.

We have been thinking so far of the arts in relation to church architecture and liturgical worship. But in fact Christianity offers us a much wider conception of worship: namely that it can find expression through every different creative activity in which men engage. The artist by his creative craftsmanship, the musician by his making of fine harmonies, the scholar by his pursuit of knowledge, the scientist by his study of the laws of Nature—all alike can make the use of their particular gifts and talents a real kind of worship, a genuine expression of their reverence and love towards God. As Clutton Brock once said:

"The Universe is to be valued because there is truth in it

and beauty in it, and we live to discover the truth and the beauty, no less than to try and do what is right."

The Christian artist or musician will not always paint religious pictures or make religious music. Far from it. But on the other hand his work will never contradict certain standards, and behind all his painting, all his music-making, there will lie his sense of the splendour and reality of God; God, the Source of all beauty, goodness and truth, the supreme Artist, Thinker, Lover. For that reason the Christian artist will never be able to acquiesce in any kind of art which is false or ugly or insincere.

Certainly great art, in all its forms, is a true tribute to God, the great Creator. More than that, at its best, art in its supreme manifestations always holds within it something of spiritual quality. That is doubtless the reason why frequently after listening to great music or watching a fine play finely performed or spending an hour in an exhibition of excellent paintings, one feels as though somehow it had been a purifying experience. I remember feeling it after seeing a splendid performance of Peer Gynt on a winter evening, or again after listening to the St. Matthew Passion one Holy Week,

What is supremely needed today is a new and greater renaissance, in which all the finer fruits of the human spirit are seen to have their common source and inspiration in God, and are used for his glory. We have talked too long about the conflict of science and religion. We have been content for too long with the divorce, or at least the separation, between art and religion. What is immensely needed now is a new alliance of friendship and mutual trust, between religion and music, art and science. Such a renaissance would result, I believe, in a wonderful enrichment of life for us all, and a broadening of culture throughout the Western hemisphere.

THE CHRISTIAN DOCTRINE OF WORK

"Be servants to one another in love."

Galatians 5: 13

There is widespread concern at this moment about a threatened strike among shipyard workers and others associated
with them. The strike is tragic and disturbing, not only because
of the hardship it will cause in many households, not only
because of its paralysing effects on one of our greatest industries;
but perhaps chiefly because it is one more evidence of unsatisfactory human relations in the industrial field. Continual
disputes, strikes, and threats of strikes in recent years plainly
shows that between employers and employed there exists a
barrier of suspicion and distrust, creating in many firms an
atmosphere of discontentment and insecurity.

It would not be right from a Christian pulpit to make any
comments or express any opinions on the rights and wrongs of
the strike itself. The particular questions involved must be
discussed round a conference table by representatives of both
sides in the dispute; and we must pray that in such a conference
a spirit of fair mindedness and charity may prevail, leading
soon to a just settlement. But if Christianity has nothing to
say on such matters, if it has no bearing on man's daily work,
on the spirit in which he does it and the rewards he may expect
from it, on the human relationships between the workers and
employers involved in it; then indeed the Christian Gospel
would be irrelevant to the concerns and responsibilities of
ordinary life, and the Christian Church could not expect that
its voice would be listened to.

Behind this strike and other similar disputes, there lie much
larger issues than the question of hours of work or a guaranteed minimum wage; issues in which all of us are in some
measure involved. And it is good that we who are Christians
should remind ourselves of certain great principles plainly
set out in Holy Scripture. It is the disregard of these principles which constitute the root cause of many of the most

serious problems in the social, economic and industrial life of the nation.

1. The first of these principles is THE DUTY OF CHARITY.

"Be servants to one another in love," says St. Paul. There is no need to enlarge upon the importance of this duty. It is not only basic to all good citizenship; it is the foundation of all proper human relationships. Charity is the cement which can bind together the diverse elements in society, with their varied interests and talents and traditions, and form a true community. Where charity is lacking, all kinds of evils break in and disrupt and embitter social life.

The most serious factor in industrial disputes is that the spirit of charity is lacking. The two sides, employers and employed, seem to regard themselves as enemies lined up for battle. Phrases like 'a fight to the finish' have been used. We are told that both sides are eager to have a 'showdown'. And behind such language lies the sinister conception (deliberately fostered in some quarters) of class warfare.

In such an atmosphere of rancour and bitterness, of arrogance and anger, there can be no possible hope of achieving reconciliation and understanding. Where men allow themselves to be animated by feelings of anger and resentment, they can no longer even see a situation in its true colours. Their judgment is warped.

The supreme need in the whole realm of industry at this moment is the putting away of suspicion and rancour, and the birth of a new spirit of charity. Only in an atmosphere of charity will any profitable approach between the two sides in a dispute become possible. St. Paul, in a famous passage from his Letter to the Corinthians, describes this Christian love: "Love is patient and kind. Love is never perverse or proud; never insolent; is not irritable; does not brood over an injury."

2. Of supreme relevance is the CHRISTIAN DOCTRINE OF WORK.

Work is thought of by many people today as an evil necessity, an unpleasant duty which has to be got through with as little trouble as possible. A man is obliged to work simply in order to earn a living. From this view, it follows that the less strenuous the work and the higher the wages, the better; the fortunate man being the man who, in army phraseology, 'holds the cushy job'.

This kind of outlook is all too common in industry today, and is distorting the whole perspective. It makes many men resentful against the necessity of work and indifferent as to the quality of work they do.

Again and again in the Old Testament there are descriptions of craftsmen skilled at some particular trade, taking pride in their work, finding satisfaction in it, and known throughout the community for their strength and skill in working with stone or wood, iron or precious metals. Work, in the writings of the Bible, is taken for granted. It is the most natural form of human activity, and it is assumed that God intends men and women to use the gifts with which he has endowed them, both for the benefit of themselves and their families and for the benefit of their neighbours and fellow citizens.

We have for too long been apt to think of vocation as only applying to certain fields of service—medicine, nursing, the ministry, the foreign mission field. It is a completely unjustifiable assumption, however, that God 'calls' a doctor, but does not call an engineer; that the foreign missionary has a divine vocation, but not a farmer or an architect. There is certainly no evidence in the Bible for this assumption. On the contrary, we find it there clearly said that God calls and equips men for all kinds of different spheres of work. In a significant passage Moses says to the Israelites:

"See the Lord hath called by name Bezallel the son of Uri, and he hath filled him with the spirit of God, in wisdom, in knowledge, and in all manner of workmanship to work in gold and in silver and in brass and in the cutting of stones to set them, and in carrying of wood to make any manner of cunning work, both he and Eholiad. Them hath he filled with wisdom of heart to work all manner of work of the engraver, and of the embroiderer in blue and in purple, in scarlet and in fine linen, and of the weaver and them that do any work."

Here plainly is the concept of Divine vocation as applying to the work, not of the prophet or the priest, but of the jeweller, the weaver, the cabinet-maker, the silversmith.

More than that, as far as possible, men and women are intended to find enjoyment in their work. In the autobiography of Dame Laura Knight, for example, we have a picture of the artist at work and the intense exhilaration which it can bring. Describing the painting of a certain picture, she says:

"I ordered a canvas 7 ft. 6 ins. by 5 ft. from Newmans. It came and was a beautiful surface and I laid out and stretched the canvas on the studio floor. The next day the canvas was in lovely condition. At 8 o'clock we started work in one of the fields. A wind had sprung up in the night. Edgar had fixed the stretcher firmly on fixed poles, but the canvas bellied in and out in the breeze.

"Dolly, the model, behaved heroically. In imagination I see her standing like a stoic hour after hour, my dark hat with its green feather on her head; on her face the mysterious smile that everyone admired so much. We were all in the tensest state, otherwise we could not have gone through the strain. Edgar made black coffee hourly, which we sipped as we stood—there were no rests. At half-past five I downed tools and cleaned up the mess. Even my hair was coated with paint. I brought the canvas into the studio, practically finished."[1]

Ideally, a man's work ought to be a kind of fulfilment of his personality. In it he ought to find scope for his powers and faculties, whether it be by alertness and ingenuity of mind or by strength and dexterity of hand. There is indeed something creative in all labour well done—in controlling a machine, in driving a bus, in ploughing a straight furrow, no less than in drafting a new Act of Parliament or designing a ship. It is true that some sorts of work are inevitably accompanied by monotony and the dullness of routine. In such jobs, it is much more difficult to keep freshness and zest alive. But they too can be illuminated by a higher motive, which can at least help to redeem the dullness.

St. Paul says: "I implore you by God's mercy to offer your very selves to him: a living sacrifice dedicated and fit for his acceptance."

That is to say, we are to dedicate our bodily powers, our strength of muscle, our skill of hand, our quickness of eye, our energy of brain, to be used for the glory of God. He the great Creator expects each one of us to do only and always our best,

---

[1] By kind permission of Peter Davies Ltd.

whatever be our field of labour and responsibility. For only the best is worthy of God.

If a cabinet-maker were asked to make a special chair, or a goldsmith to make a brooch, for the use of our beloved Queen, what infinite care they would take over every stroke of the chisel or hammer or plane; so that the quality of craftsmanship should be the finest they could produce, and prove worthy of her approval. In that fashion, says the Bible, should all our work be done, in order that it may be worthy of the approval of Almighty God.

A disturbing feature in the whole field of industry at the present time is that many of those engaged in it are more interested in the financial profits or the wage packet than in the work itself. We are living in a period in which economic values and standards tend more and more to eclipse and replace moral and spiritual standards; an age in which ambition, success and achievement are thought of almost universally in terms of money. The worship of money is an insidious danger. It can distort the whole perspective of life; blinding us alike to our duty to God and to our fellow-men. "Beware! Be on your guard against greed of every kind," says Jesus, "for even when a man has more than enough, his wealth does not give him life." The most serious fact in the field of industry today is that so many, employers and employed alike, are tempted to think of their daily work only in terms of wages and dividends.

Whereas if the Christian doctrine of work were understood and accepted by all who profess and call themselves Christian, it would transform the whole field of industry. Employer and employed alike would discover a new incentive. They would find a new satisfaction in using their knowledge and strength and skill. They might discover zest, even in mechanical, monotonous jobs. They would still be concerned about financial rewards; but they would know that the work itself is even more important than the wage. Because the work is an enterprise which they can do to the glory of God and to the benefit of their neighbour. The waiter serving his customers in a crowded restaurant, or the lighthouse keeper guarding his lamp on a lonely headland; the cashier writing figures into a ledger, or the riveter driving bolts through the hull of a ship; the schoolteacher presiding over a class of wild boys, or the district commissioner presiding over a community of backward tribes; the scientist experimenting in his laboratory with rare substances, or the dustman clearing away rubbish from the streets, or the social worker visiting in an east-end slum: each one alike can feel that his work is worthwhile. He has been called to it by God, he has been equipped for it by God; he can do it with all his might to the glory of God.

3. There is another great Christian principle which is no less relevant and important: THE VALUE OF THE INDIVIDUAL

Christianity brought for the first time into the world the doctrine that every individual man and woman, whatever his or her social status or natural ability or educational qualifications, was a person; a person infinitely precious in God's sight and therefore possessing certain inherent and inalienable rights. It has taken many centuries for this doctrine of the value of the individual to be accepted even in the countries of the West. Now at last it has been accepted, at least in theory. The rights of the human person as such have been written into the Charter of the United Nations. They received magnificent and memorable popular expression in the late President Roosevelt's 'Four Freedoms', to which every man and woman is entitled: freedom from fear; freedom from want; freedom of conscience; and freedom of worship. Here in Britain we all accept them, at least in theory, as almost axiomatic.

But, in spite of that, there still remains in the minds of thousands of people in industry the haunting fear of want. It is like a spectre, seldom seen in the full light of day, seldom talked about, but there in the background. And no one can begin to understand the contemporary problems in the field of industry who does not recognise that haunting fear. There are many older men and women who remember only too vividly the ghastly years of high unemployment, the Means Test, and the standard of living in many households at the near-poverty line.

They wish to be certain that those days never return. They want to be sure that their children will never know the meaning of poverty as they experienced it. And so they demand economic security; freedom from fear and freedom from want. That, for many men engaged in the present industrial strikes and disputes, is the cardinal issue. And there can be no hope of a satisfactory settlement until it is recognised.

In spite of the setting-up of the Welfare State, the average worker still feels that his value and his rights are under-estimated. I think he perhaps pictures the field of industry as resembling a gigantic chess-board. In the course of the game the King and the Queen, the Castle and the Knight, yes, and even the Bishop, are guarded rather carefully, are moved about with dignity, and are as far as possible sheltered from the ruder shocks of fortune. But the humble pawns are constantly moved hither and thither, have little power and prestige, and can be sacrificed without much sorrow. Even keeping this metaphor, however unsatisfactory, the pawns in industry must be recognised as having a status and inherent rights of their own.

No one can read the New Testament seriously without noticing how constantly in word and action Jesus our Lord stressed the value of the individual—the so-called Unimportant no less than the Very Important Person. In the sphere of economics and industry, that principle has still to be fully recognised and given effect to. One application of it is a recognition of the right to economic security for every person who is willing to do an honest day's work. How such security can be achieved, in spite of the inevitable fluctuations of prosperity and employment, is one of the problems that has yet to be fully solved.

"The workman earns his pay," says St. Paul. "Masters, be just and fair to your slaves, knowing that you too have a Master in heaven." And even in the Old Testament, the principle is no less plainly stated: "Woe unto him that buildeth his house by unrighteousness, that uses his neighbour's service without wages, and gives him not for his work." This principle of a just wage has always been asserted by the Christian Church, although not always acted upon, even in a Christian country like our own.

But of course the crucial question is: What, in any given social set up, constitutes a just wage? and who is to determine it? Well, it has come to be recognised that in a modern democratic society such as that of our own country, the rate of wages cannot be arbitrarily decided by either employer or employed independently of the other, nor even fairly determined by the law of supply and demand. A just wage must clearly take into account both the need of the worker and his family, and also the quality and demandingness of the work required. And where a dispute arises, some sort of negotiation is essential. No less important is it that the negotiations should be conducted in the right kind of spirit and atmosphere. It must be a meeting round a table of representatives of all concerned, where there can be frank exchange of views, where those present can try together to discover the honourable and fair solution and where, above all, an attempt can be made to establish personal relationships based on mutual respect and on a genuine desire and resolve to do and accept what is fair.

Perhaps the frequency of disputes threatening the well-being of the whole community may help to recall us to the Christian view of work as the use of our strength and our talents, our skill and knowledge, both to the glory of God who made us, and in the service of the society in which he has placed us. When this view of work is accepted, then a new atmosphere will prevail, not only in the shipbuilding yards and engineering shops, but throughout every part of our national life.

THE LAW IN A CHRISTIAN LAND

A Sermon before the Sheriffs and Members of the
Royal Faculty of Procurators of Glasgow

"Every person must submit to the supreme authorities.
There is no authority but by act of God, and the existing
authorities are instituted by him; consequently anyone
who rebels against authority is resisting a divine institution,
and those who so resist have themselves to thank for the
punishment they will receive. For government, a terror to
crime, has no terrors for good behaviour. You wish to have
no fear of the authorities? Then continue to do right and you
will have their approval, for they are God's agents working
for your good. But if you are doing wrong, then you will
have cause to fear them; it is not for nothing that they
hold the power of the sword, for they are God's agents of
punishment, for retribution on the offender."

Romans 13, verses 1-4

In the Middle Ages, when the Church had a stronger hold on
the common life than it does today, the administration of the
Law was largely in its hands. And Canon Law was the strongest and most widely recognised authority in the land. For a
purely Christian nation, such a conception would be natural.
And in a truly Christian country there ought certainly to be no
difference in general principles between the Law of the Church
and the Law of the State. Although how far, in a Christian
country, the Law of the land ought to encourage, or even
reflect, Christian ethical standards is a debatable issue.

Sad to say, we all need the restraints of the Law! Because in
almost all of us the urge of self-interest and self-aggrandisement
is so strong that some outside curb is necessary. And in almost
all of us our judgment is so apt to be darkened by prejudice
or pride or passion, that we require the guidance of some
external impartial authority to keep us fair in our thinking
and action.

Sometimes the restraints of the Law are provoking. If I am
late for an engagement and in haste to reach my destination,

it is irritating to have to drive my car at only thirty miles an hour. If I see a lovely stretch of river, and feel a powerful inclination to discover if there are any trout or salmon ready to rise to the casting of a fly, it is irritating to remember that it is private water and that there is a law against trespassing. If I am filling up my income tax return form, it is perhaps unpleasant to think that even small deviations from honesty might bring me into the Sheriff Court. Yet secretly, we all accept these troublesome restrictions upon our conduct as right and necessary.

The profession of Law is based chiefly upon the great elementary and elemental ideal of justice. Justice is not a distinctively Christian or theological virtue, like faith, hope and charity; but it is one of the cardinal virtues. Indeed, as has been truly said: "Justice is the foundation of all virtue."

The Bible lays strong emphasis upon the importance of justice. "What doth the Lord require of thee but to do justly and to love mercy" (Micah, 6: 8); "Ye shall do no unrighteousness in judgment, in meteyard, in weight or in measure. Just balances, just weights, a just ephah shall ye have. I am the Lord your God" (Leviticus 19: 35).

Now the Law of this country is based upon the ideal of justice. It may not always be successful in achieving this. There are bad laws and defective laws and inadequate laws. But a good system of Law aims at achieving justice in a community as between man and man or group and group. It is the structure by which a nation tries to secure fair dealing.

In this present sinful world in which we live, Law is essential. It plays a very important and beneficial role; chiefly perhaps in a negative sense: as a kind of moral barbed wire. Because it is a bulwark against violence and greed, against dishonesty and unscupulous selfishness.

Yet, however provoking at times such legal restraints may be, most of us recognise that the Law is a friendly guardian. Inwardly we approve of its restraints, and are grateful for its compulsive power. Because inwardly we almost all honour justice; and desire that justice should prevail throughout the community in which we live. And at the same time we almost all know that, if that is to be even approximately realised, then we need the discipline of external Law to help us.

It was a famous lawyer himself who once said that ninety-

G

nine times out of a hundred, he would buy his railway ticket even if there were no inspectors; but on the hundredth occasion, the presence of the inspector might make all the difference!

It is sometimes said that in the teaching of Jesus little stress is laid upon justice; that in fact justice has been superseded by love. But actually this is a misrepresentation. In many of our Lord's parables justice is clearly taken for granted. It is true that he tells his followers that they are to live by the royal law of love, and that their duty towards their fellow-men is not limited by the standard of what is just. "Do good and lend, without expecting any return." "Be kind to the ungrateful and wicked." "Pray for your persecutors."

Yet the teaching of Jesus clearly implies that in this present sinful world, and amid the many temptations of ordinary life, law and order must be maintained, for the good of the community as a whole. And perhaps the most perfect and complete definition of justice ever enunciated is to be found in our Lord's famous saying: "Always treat others as you would like them to treat you."

It is clear that Jesus in all his teaching assumes that men should submit to duly constituted authority, be loyal in obeying the law of the land, even when it seems harsh. Some of his followers wished him to encourage political rebellion, so that Judaea might regain its freedom. But he would have nothing to do with such a project. Even although his own countrymen are living in subjection to a great foreign power, he advises them to be quiet and peaceable. As Dr. E. F. Scott says:

"Whenever he makes reference to military discipline, courts of justice, functions of rulers, he acknowledges the rights of authority as a matter of course . . . Men are to submit to the State, acknowledging that in the present age it performs a necessary and beneficent service."

Christ's attitude to civil laws and regulations is summed up in that great saying: "Pay Caesar what is due to Caesar and pay God what is due to God."

So, too, St. Paul:

"Every subject must submit to the supreme authorities. There is no authority but by act of God, and the existing authorities are instituted by him; consequently anyone who rebels against authority is resisting a divine institution, and those who so resist have themselves to thank for the punishment they will receive . . . It is not for nothing that they hold the power of the sword, for they are God's agents of punishment, for retribution on the offender" (Romans 13: 1-4).

The Bible then teaches that God has ordained laws and authorities to administer them. As Dr. A. R. Vidler says:

". . . these apparently impersonal laws and wrathful ordin-ances, forcibly imposed, are ultimately an expression of the mercy of God. That is to say, God in His mercy has authorised the administration of civil law and order, to protect human society from the greater evils of anarchy, chaos, and ambitious dictatorship. It is the office of Law to provide a framework for human society, which has to be hard and impersonal, so that within that framework there will be scope for free, personal relationships."

This position is officially recognised in the *Articles of the Church of Scotland*:

"VI. This Church acknowledges the divine appointment and authority of the civil magistrate within his own sphere, and maintains its historic testimony to the duty of the nation acting in its corporate capacity to render homage to God, to acknow-ledge the Lord Jesus Christ to be King over the nations, to obey His laws, to reverence His ordinances, to honour His Church, and to promote in all appropriate ways the Kingdom of God. The Church and the State owe mutual duties to each other, and acting within their respective spheres may signally promote each other's welfare. The Church and the State have the right to determine each for itself all questions concerning the extent and the continuance of their mutual relations in the discharge of these duties and the obligations arising therefrom."

Yet when all this has been said, when we open the New Testament and above all when we study the words of Christ, it becomes clear that he calls his followers to live at a level far above the mere demands of the Law. Mere obedience to legal rules and prohibitions is frequently inspired only by fear. Homage to abstract ideals of justice and truth produces conduct which is correct, but cold and impersonal. For the Law can never create or inspire goodness. Justice, as demanded by the Law, is at best a civic or social virtue. Those who respect it, respect it only as a duty owed to the state or society. We who are Christians know that there is a higher sanction for right living: namely that it is a duty owed to God himself, a holy and wise God whose throne is established in righteousness. When we discover that, then the motive and inspiration for the living of the good life becomes no longer fear, but love— love of God as the supreme Source of goodness, and love of our fellow-men for his sake. So that as Paul's Letter to the Romans declares, the old Ten Commandments can all be summed up in one new commandment:

"He who loves his neighbour has satisfied every claim of the Law. For the commandments 'Thou shalt not commit adultery', 'Thou shalt not kill', 'Thou shalt not steal', 'Thou shalt not covet', and any other commandment there may be, are all summed up in the one rule, 'Love your neighbour as yourself.' Love cannot wrong a neighbour; therefore the whole Law is summed up in Love" (Romans 13: 8).

With most of us it is a very gradual process, this learning to do what is good and speak what is true, not because it is a moral obligation but because it is an expression of our loyalty to higher laws than those of any human community. But those who have begun to live by that Law of Love are set free from a merely legalistic obedience, and are already living in the "liberty of the children of God".

SPIRITUAL HEALING[1]

In any consideration of spiritual healing by Christians, it is right and proper to begin by a study of the Gospel narratives, in order to see what Christ our Lord has to say on the subject. When we open the Gospels it becomes at once clear that in the public ministry of Jesus, teaching and healing are alike prominent. The writers not only tell us again and again that, into whatever town or village he entered, sick people were brought to him and he healed them; but they give us accounts of many particular cases of cure, sometimes in considerable detail. To those who see Christ as the Incarnate Son of God, it is not surprising, far less incredible, that he should be able to perform what are usually described as miracles, happenings which cannot be explained by the ordinary, familiar 'laws of Nature', since he himself is Lord of Nature. And in the ministry of Jesus when he dwelt here among us, we Christians are convinced that we see in action the Divine purpose of love and compassion, and the Divine power to heal and restore. Wherever during his earthly ministry Jesus saw forces that threatened men's full development, peace of mind or integrity of character, he was ready to give his help.

This work of healing was carried on by the disciples of Christ after his departure as part of their mission, and through his power. And during subsequent centuries the Church has been constantly regular in its ministry of intercession for the sick. But in recent years in our own country there has been considerable interest in 'spiritual' or 'divine' healing of a more specialised kind; partly due to the activities of certain healers both within and outside the Church, partly due to the coming into existence of groups in England, and more lately in Scotland, such as the Guild of Health, the Guild of St. Raphael and the Divine Healing Mission. Although usually working independently, certain ministers have felt a special vocation to this exercise of spiritual healing, and have emphasised its importance as integral to the life and work of the Christian Church.

[1] By kind permission of *Medical News*.

While a ministry of 'spiritual healing' (so-called) may be carried on by a Minister of religion, it must be recognised that all healing is really Divine Healing, whether effected by intercession and the laying-on of hands, or by the normal methods of scientific medicine. For God is the Source of all life and health. And the doctor or the surgeon, in no less literal a sense, is the agent of God's compassion and help to those in need. Behind the intercession of the ordinary Christian and behind the scientific research, knowledge, and skill of the trained doctor alike, is the mighty curative, restorative, forgiving love of the great Father in heaven.

Which leads to a very important practical question: namely, What is the relationship, if any, between the clergyman engaged in his pastoral ministry of healing by prayer and the professional medical practitioner or medical psychiatrist?

It seems of immense importance to the great majority of clergy who have given thought and study to the subject that there should be the closest possible understanding between the doctor and the minister of religion. Too often in the past it has been assumed that each has his own province, and that neither should attempt to intrude into the domain of the other. This situation is now changing, at least in theory; but much remains to be done in practical arrangements for closer consultation and co-operation. Developments both in psychosomatic medicine and in psychiatry have shown that any such separation is unrealistic and unjustifiable. Disease is not a phenomenon which can be treated in independence of the whole personality of the individual concerned. Mind and body interact too closely. As has been said, "There are no diseases; there are only sick persons."

Medical practitioners today well recognise that fact. In a Supplement to the *British Medical Journal* of November 8th, 1947, there appeared these important statements:

"The British Medical Association Council has considered and discussed with representatives of the Churches' Council of Healing, the relationship of doctor and priest or minister in connection with their respective vocations, and the ways in which their co-operation will be of service to the community . . . The Council of the B.M.A. is of opinion that there is no ethical reason to prevent medical practitioners from co-operating with clergy in all cases, and more especially those in which the doctor in charge of the patient thinks that religious ministrations will conduce to health and peace of mind, or lead to recovery . . . Moral aspects in the cause, treatment and prevention of disease cannot be overlooked, and in this field also it is desirable that there should be fuller co-operation. Medicine and the Church working together should encourage a dynamic philosophy of health. Health is more than a physical problem, and the patient's attitude both to illness and to other problems is an important factor in his recovery and adjustment to life . . . For these reasons we welcome opportunities for discussion and co-operation in the future between qualified medical practitioners and all who have a concern for the religious needs of their patients."[1]

Within the field of modern medicine itself, as has been said, there has been in recent years a growing recognition of the intimate association and interplay of body and mind. The wise doctor, studying and taking into account, as he must, the whole personality, temperament and outlook of his patients, knows well how often their cure will depend not only on physical but on mental, moral and spiritual factors and how treatment may be either helped or frustrated by the patient's own psychological and spiritual state.

In such cases, there is obviously need for close understanding and co-operation between the doctor and the Minister of religion. Both are concerned for the welfare of the patient, body, mind and spirit. And there is ample evidence to show that prayer can be of the greatest help not only in strengthening faith, in giving serenity of mind, in removing anxiety and nervousness, but also sometimes in relieving pain.

The ministry of Spiritual Healing must however always be used with the utmost discretion and humility, and in consultation with the patient's doctor. Where such consultation and co-operation are lacking, dangerous consequences can follow. External symptoms of an illness may disappear, giving the impression of a cure, while the disease itself may remain. The patient may in this way be encouraged to imagine that the services of a doctor are no longer necessary, or may consult a doctor only when it is too late. It is vital to recognise that in any

[1] By kind permission of the *British Medical Journal*.

and every case of illness, correct diagnosis is essential, and this can only be provided by the trained and experienced medical practitioner. The inexperienced, amateur healer working independently, however good his intentions may be, can do untold harm. On the other hand, if working in consultation with the doctor, he may be able to give spiritual help quite beyond the range of scientific medicine.

Modern medical research has revealed the very close inter-action between body and mind; bad psychosomatic illness is widely prevalent. It is therefore not surprising that such cases are those which seem to offer a specially appropriate field for the ministry of spiritual healing. Nervous disorders, with their accompanying physical symptoms, are often greatly relieved by a service of Spiritual Healing; cures being frequently achieved in cases of asthma, bronchitis, skin diseases and paralysis. And it can safely be said that, in the vast majority of cases, even where physical cure is not effected, the patient is greatly bene-fited; his fears, his depression, or his resentment being removed and his peace of mind and confidence being restored.

Many illnesses are actually due to a suppressed sense of guilt or to a sense of moral weakness and frustration; and here of course what is of primary and most urgent importance is the bringing of the person concerned to acknowledge his sin, and to find spiritual restoration and peace of mind through the experience of forgiveness.

A vital factor in the ministry of spiritual healing is inter-cessory prayer.

What exactly is this prayer of intercession, and how does it work? It is the drawing of some person or persons in thought and imagination into the light and love of God's Presence. We cannot explain how this should be possible. While modern science has given us an ever-increasing understanding of the material universe and its laws, our understanding of the spiritual world and its laws is still very dim and meagre. We cannot explain even the possibility of prayer; how we finite beings, set in this sphere of earth and time, should be able to hold converse with God the Infinite Being, transcending all limitations of space and time. Still less can it be explained how by our prayers we should be able in some real fashion to help other men and women.

Yet although we cannot explain the operation of such prayer, we do know that by it we are able to help one another, and that sometimes it is the only way in which we can help. A friend visiting in a house where there is serious illness will say: "I can't do much, but I will be remembering you in my prayers." Not long ago, when visiting a man who had come through a dangerous operation in hospital, he said to me, "I know that the only thing which has enabled me to face this ordeal, and to come safely through, has been that so many people have been holding me up in their prayers."

The workings of prayer are not amenable to scientific analysis and description. There are perhaps possibilities of interaction and intercommunication of mind and spirit between one person and another, of which we know almost nothing. But the fact seems certain that somehow by our intercessions we are able to release into the world new forces of spiritual power and peace, and to help one another.

Mental illness is due to a variety of causes. They may be found in the individual's own constitution, physiological or psychological. They may be found in his heredity. Or they may be found in the influence exerted by his environment, domestic, social, material and economic. In our own time much attention has been given to the effect on health, outlook and character of bad housing, economic anxiety, or bad or strained family relationships.

It will usually require professional training and experience in psychological method to diagnose and disentangle the causes in each particular case of mental sickness. The old adage, 'a healthy mind in a healthy body', is an excellent ideal to be aimed at, and might be extended to 'a healthy mind in a healthy society'. But one of the chief tasks of those engaged in psychological medicine is to help people to adjust themselves to a given environment even when it is not ideal. Here is where the spirit can be helped to triumph.

I wonder, if, as a clergyman, I might venture to sound a note of warning or at least of questioning. Is there not a danger lest some of those concerned with mental illnesses think of cure simply in terms of what one might call psychological manipulation? Unquestionably salutary changes of outlook and modifications of thought-processes can often be effected by methods of suggestion or hypnosis or electrical treatment. And the researches and discoveries of psycho-analysis have undoubtedly thrown much new light on the workings of the human mind.

But Man is a spiritual as well as a rational being. And there can be no complete mental health for a person unless he is intellectually and emotionally adjusted to Ultimate Reality; unless that is to say, he is living in a proper relationship not only with his fellow-men but with God, the Creator, the Sustainer, the Redeemer, the Judge. We who are Christians know that the Ultimate Reality in this mysterious universe is spiritual. A man only discovers and realises his own nature and destiny through converse with God. Until, in however meagre a measure, he has entered into this spiritual supernatural relationship, he is essentially rootless and restless. In reconciliation with God, and only then, he finds mental peace and contentment, and achieves true mental health. This learning to live 'in tune with the Infinite' is the condition of any real serenity. As the great St. Augustine puts it: "Thou O God, hast made us for thyself, and our hearts are restless until they rest in thee."

Religion, that is to say, is not, as is sometimes suggested, a kind of useful 'wishful thinking'; nor is it even an optional interest for those who are mystically inclined. Religion is Man's essential adjustment to Ultimate Reality. Every man's deepest need is the need of God. For, whether he knows it or not, he owes his being to God, is dependent upon God, and at last will have to render his account to God.

Do those engaged in psychiatry, psycho-therapy and psycho-analysis, always recognise this fundamental fact about human nature? Or do they sometimes treat a sick person as though he were self-sufficient, self-subsistent? I cannot answer these questions. I only venture to raise them for consideration; and venture also to say that any mental treatment which ignores man's spiritual nature and need of religion cannot achieve complete success.

A merely humanistic or secular psychology is based on a false set of premises, and is therefore mentally and spiritually inadequate. For, to use an old-fashioned evangelical phrase, if a man is to reach inner peace and poise, he needs to be 'right' not only with his own impulses and emotions and desires, but to be 'right with God'.

Perhaps it may be asked: Is a cure always to be expected in response to prayer and the laying-on of hands? And if not, why not? It is one aspect of the whole complex problem of unanswered prayer.

In St. John's Gospel, Jesus said: "If you ask the Father for anything in my name, he will give it you." But quite clearly that is not to be thought of as a kind of spiritual blank cheque. He was speaking to his own intimate friends and disciples. They would know that that promise must always be governed by the condition that what is prayed for must be in accordance with the will and purpose of God, and moreover that we human beings, with our limited knowledge and insight, cannot fully grasp or understand the purposes of God either for our own life or for the lives of others. Even, therefore, what may seem to us reasonable requests may sometimes be refused. Certain of our prayers may remain unanswered, or at least not answered in the way we hoped.

It is especially important for those engaged in the ministry of healing to remember this. In preparing a sick person for treatment and prayer, they should never promise complete physical cure. That may or may not be given. What they do, if they are wise, is to persuade the patient to leave himself with complete trust in God's hands; realising that God "co-operates for good with those who love him".

When prayer for healing is undertaken in that spirit, there is no danger of the failure of *physical* cure leading to bitter disappointment and perhaps loss of faith. On the contrary, even if in such cases physical cure is not granted, a new sense of serenity and quietness of mind almost invariably follows. And in many instances it is found that not only anxiety and resentment, but bodily discomfort and pain are relieved. I think of a woman of faith and high character lying for eleven years on her back in increasing helplessness. She and her husband prayed steadily, but apparently in vain, for her physical recovery. Yet never for one moment have either of them faltered in their faith in God's love and their certainty that he knows best. They would, I am sure, agree with the profound words of Martin Luther:

"A Christian finds that God gives him power to bear his troubles, and to overcome them; which is just the same thing as taking his trouble away from him and making it no longer misfortune or distress, seeing it has been overcome."

III. SOME REFLECTIONS, THEOLOGICAL AND OTHERWISE

GOD THE TRANSCENDENT

"In the year that King Uzziah died, I saw the Lord sitting upon a throne, high and lifted up, and his train filled the temple. Above it stood the seraphims. Each one had six wings; with twain he covered his face, and with twain he covered his feet, and with twain he did fly. And one cried unto another and said 'Holy, holy, holy is the Lord of Hosts. The whole earth is full of his glory.' And the house was filled with smoke."

Isaiah 6: 1-4

"He answered, 'When you pray, say, "Father . . ." ' "

St. Luke 11: 2

It may appear at first sight as though there is nothing in common between the conceptions of God presented to us in these two passages. Indeed, it could be argued that they are incompatible, if not contradictory. Isaiah, like many other writers of the Old Testament, pictures God as a Being of infinite perfection, power and splendour, wholly other to men and dwelling apart in majestic isolation; a Being in whose sight the inhabitants of the earth are as grasshoppers and in whose Presence even angels veil their faces in reverence and awe. Whereas Jesus teaches us to speak of God as "Father", to think of him as concerned in all that concerns us men, and to bring to him with confidence even the homeliest of our needs and desires.

Are these different conceptions of God actually incompatible? On the contrary, both are true. The Bible asks us to keep together in our minds the thought of the majesty and transcendence of God, and the thought of the graciousness and nearness of God.

Certainly the idea of transcendence is not popular today. As a recent writer says:

"We are living in an age when the transcendent is either widely denied or not confidently affirmed . . . It is supposed that we are imprisoned for life within the confines of human experience and that this experience can never include an experience of the transcendent. It is said that we can never understand the idea of the transcendent because it lies beyond the forms of thought or categories in which alone we are able to understand what is capable of being understood. We can have no idea of it . . . And even if we could form an idea of the transcendent, we cannot prove that it exists, because it lies outside the realm in which we can devise proofs and organise tests. We cannot know what it is, and we cannot prove that it is."[1]

In other words, there are those who deny, or at least question, the very possibility of knowledge of God, if indeed there can be any reality corresponding to the concept of God. This argument may at first sight seem plausible, in fact, logically unanswerable. But it is only unanswerable because it begs a very large question. If God is beyond the range of all possible human experience, then of course men cannot either know of him, or come into any sort of intercourse with him. But we cannot legitimately be asked to accept the first premise as axiomatic. Indeed, throughout the whole course of history, there have been great numbers of persons who have claimed that religious experience is not only a possibility, but a fact; in every generation there have been many who were convinced that they had some contact, however fleeting, some glimpse, however fragmentary, of the transcendent God, such as was granted to the prophet Isaiah in his vision.

Whatever be the arguments advanced by speculative theology for abandoning the concept of a transcendent God, for a Christian it is not permissible to discard biblical theology. To do so is ultimately to deny the possibility of revelation. For Christian thinkers, the biblical writings must be the primary and chief source of truth about spiritual realities. Otherwise the Christian thinker becomes completely airborne on the wings of his own speculative intellect, and loses contact with those historic events in which the Christian Faith is rooted.

The Old Testament writers, prophets and poets alike, had a profound sense of the transcendent majesty and holiness of God. For them he is the originator and sustainer of all things visible and invisible, upon whose providence all living creatures

[1] George Frederick Woods in *Soundings*. By kind permission of the Cambridge University Press.

depend. He is the supreme Judge of men and nations. He is the great Lawgiver whose commandments all must obey and whose authority all men must recognise. In his sight men know themselves to be finite and frail, and when they attempt to come into his Presence they are overcome by a sense of reverence and awe. It is significant that in the vision of Isaiah the temple was filled with smoke.

This recognition of ultimate mystery is an essential element in the religious approach. "Canst thou by searching find out God?" asks Job derisively. It is fashionable today to discuss God as though he could be a proper object of thought and debate. But we shall search in vain for any scientific or logical proof of God's existence. "The Eternal One is not a natural object on which we can focus our telescopes or microscopes." Nor need we ever expect to find God at the end of a philosophical argument. The greatest thinkers have indeed always recognised that any human concept of the transcendent is utterly inadequate; that God is greater than our longest thoughts or imaginings. "My thoughts are not your thoughts, neither are your ways my ways, saith the Lord."

Meister Eckhart says:

"Why dost thou prate of God? Whatever thou sayest of him is untrue."

And St. Augustine writes:

"There is in the mind no knowledge of God except the knowledge that it does not know him."

To say that God is transcendent is not so much to say that he is inaccessible as to recognise that the finite human mind can never hope to understand him. Our thoughts of him must always, as it were, run out into impenetrable mystery. It is true that the theologians have attempted the impossible task. The formulators of doctrine and dogma have endeavoured to define the nature and purposes of God, within the formulas of a creed or confession. But usually in doing so they have had recourse to language which in itself inevitably fails to express the inexpressible. *The Westminster Confession*, for example, offers this statement about the Being of God:

"There is but one living and true God, who is infinite in being and perfection, a most pure spirit, invisible, without body, parts, or passions, immutable, immense, eternal, in-comprehensible, almighty, most wise, most holy, most free, most absolute, working all things according to the counsel of his own immutable and most righteous will for his own glory, most loving, gracious, merciful, long-suffering, abundant in goodness and truth, forgiving iniquity, transgression and sin, the rewarder of them that diligently seek him, and withal most just and terrible in his judgments, hating all sin and who will by no means clear the guilty.

"God hath all life, glory, goodness, blessedness, in and of himself; and is alone in and unto himself all-sufficient, not standing in need of any creatures which he hath made, not deriving any glory from them, but only manifesting his own glory, in, by, unto, and upon them; he is the alone fountain of all being, of whom, through whom, and to whom, are all things, and hath most sovereign dominion over them, to do so by them, for them, or upon them, whatsoever himself pleaseth. In his sight all things are open and manifest; his knowledge is infinite, infallible, and independent upon the creature, so as nothing is to him contingent or uncertain. He is most holy in all his counsels, in all his works, and in all his commands. To him is due from angels and men, and every other creature, whatsoever worship, service or obedience he is pleased to require of them."

It was perhaps presumptuous to dare to put into words such a definition or description of the indefinable and indescribable. Human language is utterly inadequate. But even in such an attempted verbal statement there can be recognised the sense of mystery. For the writers knew that they were referring to that Being who transcends all human thought and imagina-tion, no less than all human words. Not the acceptance of mystery, but the arrogant refusal to recognise mystery in ulti-mate realities, keeps men from the profounder insights and experiences.

In the writings of the Bible this thought of the transcendent power and majesty of God is constantly stressed. "I saw the Lord sitting upon a throne, high and lifted up; and his train filled the temple." "Have ye not known, have ye not heard, it is he that sitteth upon the circle of the earth, that stretcheth out the heavens as a curtain and spreadeth them out as a tent

H

to dwell in, that bringeth the princes to nothing. He maketh the judges of the earth as vanity." "Clouds and darkness are round about him; righteousness and judgment are the habitation of his throne."

He is shown as the Lord of Creation. Through all the writings of the Bible there lies implicit the thought that God is the controller of the whole system of Nature. He created this whole mysterious universe. It is due to his creative power that all creatures have being. It is by his Providence that all things are sustained. The immeasurable tracts of outer space are still part of his domain. "In the beginning, God created heaven and earth." And the very idea of creation presupposes a transcendent God.

The Bible writers also show us God as the Lord of history. The nations are ultimately under his control. There is a great note which sounds through all the pages of Holy Scripture: the sovereignty of God. This proclamation runs through the Bible from the first page to the last: the conviction that God is the eternal King of the universe, that he not only once created it, but that he rules, he sustains, he controls it from generation to generation, that all power is ultimately in his hands. "The Lord sitteth King for ever." "The Lord reigneth; he is clothed with majesty." This faith in the sovereignty of God was, alike for the Old Testament and the New Testament writers, one of the supreme final convictions. Their religion took its strength from that thought; and its amazing calm and assurance, even through otherwise bewildering events. Whatever they or others did, or failed to do; whatever blunderings and mistakes men might make, yet men had not the last word. There was one who sat King over all and in whose hands was supreme power; whether through terror or gentleness, whether in periods of prosperity, or in periods of tragedy and catastrophe, he was working out his own Divine purposes on earth.

No less plainly do we find in the New Testament this same thought of God as the Lord of history. Supremely in the death and resurrection of Christ are God's mighty acts and irresistible power visible. Moreover, Jesus seems clearly to have accepted the traditional belief of the Jewish apocalyptic writings that, however sinister the forces of evil may be, however tragic the sins and follies of mankind, in the end God will show his strong hand and vindicate his supremacy, putting all evil forever under his feet. It is the conception not only of a God voluntarily involved in the processes of history, but of a trans-cendent God in control of history, and himself outside the time process.

When one turns to the teaching of Christ himself, the recogni-tion of the transcendence of God is still to be found. It is true that Jesus always speaks of God as "Father" and that he en-couraged his followers to speak to God as "our Father in Heaven". For he taught that the fundamental quality in the Being and providential activity of God is love. But it is a "love that moves the sun and all the stars". It is the love of one in whose hands is all power in heaven and earth. We men are never entitled to take any liberties with God. The modern tendency in some quarters to think of God as a kind, elderly neighbour, benevolent and understanding, who can be counted upon to be indulgent towards our human peccadillos and weaknesses, can find no justification in the teaching of Jesus. On the contrary he makes the demand for an absoluteness of obedience and self-surrender, which is formidable beyond words as soon as we discover it.

In the life, and work, and death, and resurrection of Christ himself there are strange but unmistakable intimations and undertones of transcendence. Even his own disciples never completely understood him. The supreme instance of this is the transfiguration. In that strange experience on the hilltop the Master who was the familiar companion of their days was suddenly revealed to his followers in an aspect of mystery and remoteness. Again, at the Last Supper, in the upstairs room the night before his death, the writer of the fourth Gospel tells us that in utter humility Jesus took a towel to wash the feet of his disciples knowing "that he had come from God and was going back to God". Once again the sense of the transcendent sud-denly invading the sphere of the homely and intimate.

Here are unmistakable intimations of a power from beyond the range of human experience and comprehension.

There has been a curious attempt in certain theological circles recently to deny the transcendence of God. We are told that it is mistaken to think of God as "up there" or "out there" or as "beyond". We are to find him rather in the depth of our own being and in our human relationships and our traffic with the secular world. There is truth in this, but only partial truth. For the insight of the biblical writers has always insisted both on the transcendence and on the nearness of God. He is both a God who sits in unique sovereignty over his creation and a God who reveals himself within his created universe.

He is Lord of history, Master of men and nations. But he makes himself known in history. We men could never find him of ourselves, but he shows himself to us, he speaks to us, he comes close to us. How do we know that? How can we believe that? Because at a certain moment in history a Man lived and died and conquered death; and looking at him, Jesus of Nazareth, in all his human perfection, his courage and gentleness, his strength and his compassion, men realised that they were seeing into the very heart of Almighty God; realised that the God who was Lord of history was also involved in history, that the transcendent God Ruler of the universe was also Everyman's Friend and Helper. Dr. J. S. Whale has finely expressed it:

"The most high God, though transcending his creation is nevertheless nigh to men. He comes upon them 'from a distance' as it were, through his power or spirit. Just as the wind from the desert steppes in distant Siberia comes and breaks down the elm branches close to me here in a College court in East Anglia, so God who is infinitely remote in the ontological sense, is nevertheless experienced as ontologically near, coming upon human life and controlling it, creatively and re-creatively."

A consideration of the transcendence of God reminds us surely that we need never hope or expect to eliminate the element of mystery or the unexplainable. It is, at least under the conditions of human life on this earth, a very part of our religious faith. In entering into the profoundest experiences open to man, in looking at the highest truths revealed, we must expect to find mystery, realities beyond the reach of human reason.

It is true that the 'modern mind' has little patience with mystery. Many people feel in some vague fashion that the element of the transcendent, the unexplainable, is a weakness in Christianity. This prejudice against what is called the supernatural in religion is very strong today; not only outside the Church among its hostile critics, but also within the Church among some of its own members. Perhaps more than any other factor, it tends to weaken the authority and influence of the

Church in many quarters. The claim underlying this rational-istic attitude towards religion is virtually the claim that the human mind can understand and explain even the highest religious truths and profoundest religious experiences. Those who make this claim refuse to rest in mystery of any kind. They will not believe unless they can understand. In other words, they attempt to make faith identical with reason.

Yet, take the supernatural, the transcendent, out of Christi-anity, and it is robbed of its essential power and appeal. As George Tyrrell said:

"If we cannot save huge chunks of transcendentalism, Christianity must go. Civilisation can do (and has done) all that the purely immanental Christ of Matthew Arnold is credited with. The other-world emphasis, the doctrine of immortality, was what gave Christianity its original impulse and sent martyrs to the lions."

In fact, mystery surrounds our little lives on all sides; the great primaeval mysteries of birth and suffering and death. Even in the world of animate Nature, mystery still dwells; no one has yet explained the essence of life, or intelligence, or defined their exact boundaries. How much more should we not expect mystery in the unseen realm of spirit, in the eternal purposes of God, in the dealings of God with the human soul, in those regions and experiences where one is on the threshold, as it were, of two worlds, and the influences and gleams of the eternal break in upon earth and time. St. Augustine, meditat-ing on the mystery of God's inner life, the Blessed Trinity, saw, as in a vision, a small boy playing on the sands by the seashore. In a dry place he had made a hole and into it kept pouring bucket after bucket of water from the ocean. "I am trying to empty the sea into my hole," he said. "O my boy, you could not manage that, if you go on forever," said the onlooker. "'Twould be easier, though, than to put all the infinite mystery of the Holy Trinity into a man's mind." It is essential that we mortals, pondering on great matters, should preserve an end-less reverence and humility; like the holy seraphim, veiling our faces and bowing our heads before mysteries too dazzling for us to look upon. 'Now we see only puzzling reflections in a mirror, but then we shall see face to face'."

GOD THE OMNIPRESENT

"O that I knew where I might find . . . God!"

Job 23: 3

"O Lord thou hast searched me and known me. Thou
knowest my down-sitting and mine up-rising . . . Thou
compassest my path and my lying down and art acquainted
with all my ways."

Psalm 139: 1-2

This remarkable Psalm is the testimony of a man who has had
the supreme experience open to any human-being; he has come
into touch with the living God.

There are many people in our time who declare that they
find it impossible even to believe in the existence of God. They
point to the tidy, mathematical formulas of the scientist in his
description of the universe. Or they point to the strange,
meaningless medley of events that we call history. And they
say neither the picture of the cosmos presented to us by modern
science nor an impartial study of the course of human history
down the ages seems to show any convincing evidence of the
existence of an infinite, unseen, almighty Architect and Controller. And when it comes to an argument, or a television
debate, it often seems that the atheist has the best of it. His cold
logic seems unconquerable and the secular humanist seems to
triumph over the mystic, or the Christian believer.

But if there are people today who find it difficult to believe
in the existence of God, there is a still larger number who find
it difficult to be conscious of the reality of God. He is hardly
more than a word found in the Bible or the Apostles' Creed;
perhaps a useful religious symbol representing an unfathomable
mystery. For others, God is a philosophical concept, an abs-
truse idea to be debated about in academic groups or youth
discussion circles. But after all the debating, they do not feel
that they have 'found God'.

There are of course a great many people in our time who
scarcely ever give a thought to God, and make no attempt to
find him. But there are also many men and women who, while
perhaps never practising any of the religious observances and

having no link with the Church, are yet conscious that something is missing from their lives. They possess many things; they enjoy many things; but in their heart they know that somehow the Greatest Thing has not yet come within their reach. For all their struggles and all their success, they have not found the pearl of great price. Outwardly, so far as friends and acquaintances can judge, they are content. And yet beneath that superficial contentment, in the secret centre of their being, there is a deep unsatisfied longing: "O, that I knew where I might find —God!"

One hears the echo of that longing in a good many contemporary novels. One sees (I think) the evidences of it in much contemporary painting. One can perhaps detect signs of it in the restlessness, the rebelliousness, the unhappiness of many younger people. Doubtless 'the angry young man' is angry with society because of the evils and injustices that it permits; angry with statesmen and politicians and the Establishment because of the intolerable mess into which they have allowed the world to drift; angry with the older generation because of their lack of understanding and sympathy and common sense. But I believe that (whether he knows it or not) the 'angry young man' is also angry with himself because he has not managed to adjust himself to life and to the harsh facts of life, and above all because he has not managed to adjust himself to the Supreme Reality in the universe; and because in his innermost being something is crying out: "O, that I knew where I might find— God!"

Perhaps even some of us who do say our prayers regularly, as we were brought up to do, frequently feel that the God to whom we pray is infinitely far off, so that our words are spoken, as it were, into the unknown world of outer space. God is not 'real' to us, like the tree waving its branches in the wind outside our window, or the cat curled up on the hearth-rug at our feet, or the doctor whom we occasionally visit in his consulting room, or even the unknown Member of Parliament to whom we may feel moved to write about some troublesome problem.

Perhaps part of the difficulty is due to a wrong approach. We look to intellectual conviction rather than spiritual experience. As Dr. H. A. Happold says:

"At the heart of religious experience there is a paradox. Men of spiritual insight are, in the depths of their souls, conscious of a Presence, which they call God, and this Presence is more real to them than anything else they know. They are not, however, able to describe It as other things can be described nor do they know It as they know other things. They are compelled to say that, in terms of the human intellect, God, since He cannot be compreheded by the rational faculty, is unknown and unknowable. That, however, is only half the picture . . .

He of whom the mind can have no knowledge can be known in the deep centre of the soul. He who is neither perceptible to the senses nor conceivable by the intellect is sensible to the heart.''[1]

In this hundred-and-thirty-ninth Psalm, for example, we find the writer saying that to him God is the greatest Reality in the world and the supreme Reality in his own life. Near, every moment of every day. Through hours of darkness no less than hours of daylight. Near to us not only when we think of him but when we forget him. The Great Unseen Companion; whose Presence is always with us, like the very air we breathe.

"Thou hast beset me behind and before, and laid thine hand upon me.
Thou compassest my path.
When I awake, I am still with thee."

More than that: the writer of this Psalm says not only that God is nearer to him than any human-being, but that God understands him better than any human-being.

No other person really understands us completely. There are feelings, thoughts, longings, regrets, desires so subtle that we cannot share or communicate them. There are some things so personal, so private, that we do not wish to share or communicate them. So that converse with our neighbours, our acquaintances, our friends, yes, even our nearest and dearest, always has a touch of reserve.

But, says this Psalmist, there is one Person who understands me utterly, without any words spoken. Sees me exactly as I am: my faults and failures, my meannesses and foolishness, my

[1] By kind permission of the Cambridge University Press.

longings and aspirations. We like our neighbours to think us better than we are. We hope they won't notice our failings. We try to hide our deepest thoughts and desires from the world behind barriers of conventional speech and behaviour.

But, says this writer, no man can hide from God. He made us and he knows us, each one. When we become conscious of his Presence, then there is no room left for pretence. We can erect no barrier of reserve between him and us. He sees us as we are. "O Lord, thou hast searched me and known me. Thou understandest my thoughts afar off. There is not a word in my tongue but thou knowest it altogether."

I suppose that is what people felt when they came into the Presence of Christ; whether it were a worldly tax-collector or an arrogant Pharisee, whether a woman of the streets, or a respected town councillor. He saw them as they really were. He understood them as no one else understood them; knew the worst, but knew also the best in them. "He needed not that any should tell him, because he knew what was in man!" It was for that reason that Christ possessed a unique power to help, to comfort, to change, to restore men and women in their endless different needs.

The discovery which this mystic of the ancient world had made is the supreme discovery that any man can make: that amongst all the changing experiences of life, in all its different situations and moods, the great encompassing Presence and Providence of God is about us men; God the unseen Father and Friend, who created us, who understands us utterly, who cares for us endlessly, to whom we can turn at any moment in perfect confidence or trust. Prayer then becomes, not a routine religious duty, not a wistful reaching out into the unknown, but a conversation with One who is closer to us than even the most intimate of human-beings.

Nor is this experience of the reality and the nearness of God only for mystics and saints and very pious people. It is no less open to ordinary people in their ordinary workaday lives; people it may be not peculiarly gifted in piety at all. A visitor travelling in a remoter part of Ireland tells how he overtook an old peasant woman carrying a bucket of water, and climbing a steep stretch of road on to the moor, he took her bucket, and they fell into conversation. He discovered that all her children were long since scattered. Soon they came in sight of a cottage standing far from any other habitation. "Who lives there?" asked the traveller. And at once came the answer: "Why, 'tis God and myself."

I think of an old-age pensioner whom I used to visit frequently, a fine godly woman, half-paralysed and never able to go out, even to do her own messages. She had children and grand-children, but they hardly ever came to visit her; and almost all day she sat alone in her single-roomed house. But once, when I was sitting talking to her, she suddenly said, with complete naturalness and simplicity, "Although I am by myself all day long, I never feel alone. Because somehow I feel God is with me here, in my own small room."

"Thou hast beset me behind and before, and laid thine hand upon me. When I awake, I am still with thee."

God is everywhere, and so we can find him anywhere. Near to us in church, but no less near to us in the bus, in the noisy office or workshop, in the silence of our own room, or out on the hill or by the river bank. For most of us perhaps it is not easy to believe that. We are so prone to localise God. To think of him as shut up in church. Or shut up in Sunday. Or shut up in the fifteen minutes of our morning or evening prayer. Actually God isn't shut up anywhere within special cells, whether of space or time. He is everywhere; accessible at all times and in every place. Samuel Rutherford found him in his prison room. David Livingstone found him in the jungle of darkest Africa. Captain Scott found him amongst the blizzards of the Antarctic.

We who are Christians can know God more fully and more intimately than even the writer of this wonderful Psalm. Because in the life and person of Jesus Christ, God showed himself to men and women as never before. Showed himself as a Man; a Man living on this earth as you and I have to live. So that when we look at Jesus, we know something of the very nature and character of God. "No man has seen God at any time. But the only begotten Son, who is in the bosom of the Father, he has declared him." What is God like? I suppose we have all asked that question at some time. God is like Jesus—that is the message of Christianity.

That is why we Christians, more easily than others, ought to find it possible to believe in God, to be conscious of the reality of God, to worship God, to draw near to God in prayer and Sacrament. Yes, and even in the midst of our daily work, as Père Teilhard de Chardin suggests:

"Our work appears to us, in the main, as a way of earning our daily bread. But its essential virtue is on a higher level: through it we complete in ourselves the subject of the divine union; and through it again we somehow make to grow in stature the divine term of the One with whom we are united, Our Lord Jesus Christ. Hence whatever our role as men may be, whether we are artists, working men or scholars, we can, if we are Christians, speed towards the object of our work as though towards an opening on to the supreme fulfilment of our being. Indeed, without exaggeration or excess in thought or expression—but simply by confronting the most fundamental truths of our faith and of experience, we are led to the following observation: God is inexhaustibly attainable in the TOTALITY of our action."[1]

Yet there is also another truth, which must never be forgotten. We who are Christians have no monopoly of God or of the experience of God's reality and presence. Those of other religions, Buddhists, Hindus, Muslims, Animists—one and all are reaching out also towards God. "The heathen in his blindness bows down to wood and stone," says the familiar hymn. Yes, but even in his blindness he, too, is reaching out towards that God whose name he does not know, but of whose reality he is dimly conscious.

But one must surely go further still. There is a strange truth of which the philosopher Dr. Paul Tillich spoke in a broadcast Address:

"God is not only the God of those who are able to pray to him. He is also the God of those who are separated from him, who do not know his name, and are not able to speak to him or even about him. He is not only the God of the religious people, but he is also the God of those who reject religion."

Did the writer of this hundred-and-thirty-ninth Psalm have a glimpse of that strange truth when he wrote:

"If I make my bed in hell, behold thou art there. If I take

[1] *Le Milieu Divin.* By kind permission of Wm. Collins & Sons (Publishers).

the wings of the morning and dwell in the uttermost parts of
the sea, even there shall thy hand lead me, and thy right hand
shall hold me."

How can we, who live in the materialistic twentieth century
become more conscious of the reality and the nearness of God?
Here are some words of counsel for Christians written in the
last century by a devout priest of the Eastern Orthodox Church,
Father John of Cronstadt:

"On rising from your bed, say: 'In the Name of the Father,
the Son, and the Holy Ghost, I begin this new day'. While
washing, say: 'Purge me from my sins. Wash thou me and I
shall be whiter than snow'. When putting on your clean linen,
say: 'Create in me a clean heart, O Lord, and clothe me with
the fine linen which is the righteousness of the saints'. When you
break your fast, think of the length of Christ's fast, and in his
name eat your morning meal with gladness of heart. If you
wish to walk or drive, or go somewhere in a boat, first pray to
the Lord to keep this your going out and coming in. If you are
a scholar or an official or an officer or a painter or a manufac-
turer or a mechanic, remember that the science of sciences to
you is to be a new creature in Christ Jesus. And every day and
in every place work at the new creation which you yourself
are."

Let the last word come from a seventeenth-century monastery
from Brother Lawrence, a lay brother, working day by day in
the racket of the kitchen among the pots and pans:

"To be with God there is no need to be continually in church.
We may make an oratory of our heart in which to retire from
time to time, and with him hold humble and loving converse.
Everyone can converse closely with God. Lift up your heart to
him, even at your meals, or when you are in company. You
need not cry very loud, he is nearer to us than we think.
Accustom yourself to beg his grace, to offer him your heart
from time to time throughout the day's business, even every
moment if you can. The time of business does not with me differ
from the time of prayer. And in the noise and clatter of my
kitchen, while several people are calling for different things at
the same time, I possess God in as great tranquillity as if I were
upon my knees at the Blessed Sacrament."

WHAT IS MAN?

"What is man, that thou art mindful of him? Or the son
of man, that thou visitest him?"   Psalm 8: 4

The writer had perhaps stepped out of his door on a winter's
night, clear and touched with frost; looked up at the stars in
their myriads, at the clouds moving across the infinite dome of
the sky, the moon riding among them. And as his imagination
is baffled by the majesty and the mystery of it all, he exclaims,
"What is man, and what is man's place in this mysterious
universe?"

The Shorter Catechism has the same question. "What is
man's chief end?": a question as old as the human race, and as
new as a boy picking up the morning newspaper and reading
of the latest missile released into outer space.

While this question, "What is Man?" is ultimately a theological question. it is a question which a great many others
than theologians are being driven to ask, perhaps especially in
our time. Here, for example, are some words, not of a philosopher or theologian, but of a distinguished contemporary
scientist:

"Man has now reached a point at which his knowledge of
the evolutionary process has enabled him to begin defining
his own place in it, or starting on a scientific exploration of his
destiny."

The biologist probing ever more deeply into the mystery of
life; the engineer finding himself capable of pressing a button
unleashing the unimaginable resources of nuclear power; the
novelist watching men and women in their infinite variety of
behaviour in every kind of different situation and relationship;
the sociologist and psychiatrist pondering on the proper order
of human society, or the strange vagaries of the human mind;
the physicist becoming constantly more aware of the vast
magnitude and splendour of the universe—all, from their
different angles, are constrained to ask that same question:
"What is Man? and what is Man's place in the Cosmos?"

What kind of creature is this man, with his stupidity and cleverness, his cowardice and his courage, his loves and his hates, his
selfishness and his power of sacrifice, his earthiness and car-
nality, and his occasional reaching out towards something
beyond the earthy and carnal? "This forked radish with a head
fantastically carved," as Thomas Carlyle described him.

The same kind of questions lie implicit in a good deal of
contemporary literature. One need only think of the writings
of Albert Camus, Francois Mauriac, Graham Greene, Patrick
White, Samuel Beckett, Franz Kafka.

Sometimes the writer, through his characters, suggests an
answer to the question. More often he obviously has no
answer, and is either baffled or cynical.

When we try to consider what are the distinctive characteristics of man which, as it were, mark him out from the rest of
creation, many different replies can of course be given.

You can say, Man is a maker of language. Some of the animals may appear to communicate. There is often a good deal
of chattering in a monkey-house. But generally speaking,
beyond actions and signs and noises, animals seem to have no
way of communicating feelings or desires, still less ideas. Man
is the only real maker of language.

You can say, Man is a maker of machines. Archaeologists
and anthropologists have shown that one of the marks of even
early prehistoric man was that he forged for himself imple-
ments of stone, wood and iron. Until through the centuries he
has shown himself able to create tools and machines almost
magical in their ingenuity and terrifying in their power.

You can say, Man is a maker of ideas. He can think. He can
think in abstract terms. He can think about his own life and
the universe and speculate about meanings and concoct
arguments. He is a rational being.

You can say, Man is a social being, trying, although not
always successfully, to live in community with his fellows; and
through that community life creating new organisations. As
J. S. Huxley put it:

"Man is the sole representative of a new realm or grade of
being, equivalent in importance to all the rest of the animal
kingdom. In this sector, evolution is no longer purely biological,
but primarily cultural. What evolves is not (or is only to a

limited extent) gene systems and bodily organisations, but human cultures, social institutions, laws, arts, sciences, educational systems, techniques, codes of morals."

Or once again, you can say, Man is a recogniser of values. To many people this capacity to recognise values is the most distinctively human attribute. Men and women possess it of course in different degrees. But all men seem able, in some degree, for example, to appreciate beauty: whether in a landscape or a picture, a piece of sculpture, or a flower, or a human face. So too, all men, unless depraved or abnormal, recognise the demandingness of truth and the value of knowledge. Truthfulness in speech is the presupposition of all relationships and co-operation between human beings. The discovery of the true structure of the system of Nature is the goal of all scientific research and investigation. So too, in varying degree, all men recognise goodness when they see it. And most people recognise also its rightful demand upon them. The philosopher Kant said that the idea of absolute obligation was the most distinctive and universal mark of humanity.

Yet the Bible says there is still something more which is distinctive of Man: and it is the most important thing of all! Man is a being who reaches out towards God, who carries in his innermost being the instinct of worship, the capacity to know and hold converse with God.

Travellers and explorers tell us that wherever they journey, even among the most primitive tribes and peoples, they discover some belief in higher beings, or at least in an unseen spiritual world towards which men and women reach out in supplication and awe, in wonder or in fear. The great religions of the world—Christianity, Hinduism, Islam—all testify to this instinct of worship. Unexpected people testify to it.

H. G. Wells says in one of his books: "At times in the silence of the night and in rare lonely moments, I experience a sort of communion with Something Great that is not myself."

That Something Great is of course him whom we name God. And the most remarkable thing about Man is that he can have fellowship with God. God meets us, shows himself to us, speaks to us, allows us to speak to him. The whole history of religion through the ages proclaims that fact. The most splendid thing that happens in a town or a countryside is when a church bell rings out and men and women gather for worship, deliberately lifting up their hearts and thoughts beyond earthly things. Here is Man at his highest level of life. As Dr. Emil Brunner says:

"God created Man in such a way that he can receive God's Word. Man really becomes Man when he perceives something of God . . . We are human in the degree we permit God to speak to us. We are men only when God's Word finds an echo in us . . . Were God to cease speaking to us, we would then have ceased to be men.

It is of course true that some thinkers today are suggesting that religion is being outgrown and replaced by science. But the evidences for such an assertion seem very slight. Those who hold such a belief are a small body of intellectuals in certain Western countries. To deny the reality of a supernatural realm of being beyond the range of sensory perception or scientific investigation is to reject the validity of all mystical experience through the long centuries of history. It is also to deny what appears to be a fundamental element in the human make-up. Moreover, the great mass of mankind still hold to belief in spiritual reality. It is significant that in this scientific twentieth century we are still building cathedrals as well as nuclear power stations.

It is in religion that man finds the meaning both of the universe and of his own place in it. J. S. Huxley, in a striking essay, says:

"It is our business as men to discover and realise new and richer possibilities for life, and greater degrees of fulfilment for ourselves and for the evolutionary process of which man is now the spearhead. This is our privilege but also our grave and almost frightening responsibility. This at once leads to the question: 'What do we mean by fulfilment?' "

He goes on to suggest a tentative answer:

"To adopt fulfilment as our essential aim has many implications. It implies reform of our educational systems and principles: more prestige, and more money for education. It implies that society should be so organised as to provide opportunity for the fulfilment of its individual members—through adventure and meditation, through the arts and travel and shared activities. It implies the attempt to understand more about man's inner life. How can Man resolve psychological conflict, how attain inner peace and spiritual harmony?"

All very true and interesting as far as it goes. But I suggest that there can be no true fulfilment for Man, whether in this twentieth century or any other, which fails to recognise that Man is by his very nature a spiritual being. Educational reform is important; but by itself it is not enough. Adventure and meditation, the arts and travel, are not enough.

In a very ancient book, we are told that as the great grazier and cattle owner, Abraham, moved about across the prairie seeking good pasture for his flocks and herds, wherever he sojourned "there he builded an altar". A very significant fact. Modern Man too, if he is to have any sense of fulfilment, any sense of abidingness in a world of change, must build an altar—even although he can scarcely name the God he dares to worship.

Come back to the Shorter Catechism. "What is Man's Chief End?" "Man's chief end is to glorify God and to enjoy him forever." When we have discovered that, then we have discovered the real meaning of life. That is why the most important thing in the world, for any of us, is to learn to pray, and so to give God an entrance into our lives. Then everything else falls into place.

Men call God by many different names: the Absolute, the Uncaused Cause, the Transcendent, the Eternal One, the Creator, the Ultimate Source and Ground of all Being. They hold in their minds many different images of him. No image entertained by the human mind can be adequate. But he who beyond all others was the Man, the proper Man, the only one who has shown us human life and character in their full perfection, taught us to call God by a name so familiar that the most simple and the most learned alike can use it: Father. Here is the Christian name for God. And when all the philosophers have had their say, that is still his Name. "Teach us how to address God", they asked. And he replied, "When you pray, say 'Father'."

Men make touch with God in many different ways—sometimes deliberately, sometimes unexpectedly. One thing

I

seems fairly certain: you needn't expect to find God at the conclusion of an argument. Indeed, we men don't find God at all. He finds us. He shows himself to us. He is perhaps suddenly 'there', and we never suspected it; in the street, at our daily work, at a moment of danger or crisis, in the examination hall.

As I began by quoting a scientist, I finish by leaving with you the words of another scientist:

"Every man of us has a shy and lonely thing in his heart which he dare not lose, on pain of no longer being a man. One does not often speak of it, and then only softly; but since you ask a friend, I will say that it is in the Holy Communion that God is nearest and most real to me. Under the forms of bread and wine, God touches me and feeds me. How it can be so I do not know; I only know it is so. Would that I were more worthy of such a blessing; but if I were I should not need it."

JESUS: THE PROPER MAN

"You shall give him the name Jesus (Saviour), for he will save his people from their sins."   St. Matthew 1: 21

"There is no other name under heaven granted to men, by which we may receive salvation."   Acts 4: 12

A name is a significant thing. It not only helps us conveniently to refer to a particular person in speech, or writing, but it also carries with it the recognition that every human being is a distinct personality. He or she has his or her own special identity. There may of course be several people called by the same name, because obviously there aren't enough names invented to give us each a separate one. But every Thomas or John or Mary or Caroline has, in the thoughts of their friends, a special and definite identity. So that a name is a recognition of personality.

This is specially true, or true in a special kind of way, for Christians. Because when a child of Christian parents is baptised, his or her name is as it were dedicated and sanctified by being spoken in association with the great Name of God, Father, Son and Holy Ghost. That is why we often speak of someone's 'Christian name'. My 'Christian name' is the name by which I was called at my Baptism.

In the very early days of Christianity, before the Trinitanian formula had come into use, it is probable that people were simply baptised "into the name of Jesus Christ". When, after his tremendous sermon on the Day of Pentecost, the people surged round Peter and asked: "What must we do?" he answered: "Repent and be baptised, every one of you, in the name of Jesus the Messiah". "That name which," as St. Paul says, "is above any title of sovereignty that can be named, not only in this age but in the age to come."

To the Jews, the name of someone prominent was very significant, because it implied the authority or power of the person referred to. And so in everything they did the early

Christians appealed to the power and authority of Jesus their Lord and Master. It was in the name of Jesus that they healed the sick; in his name that they exorcised evil spirits; in his name they performed miracles; in his name they preached and taught; into his name converts were baptised.

"You shall give him the name Jesus; for he will save his people from their sins." "There is no other name granted to men by which we may receive salvation."

Jesus was a common name in Palestine in the first century. When the boy Jesus wrote his name on an exercise at school, it would have looked quite ordinary. When his Mother came to the door, and saw him playing with other children in the village street at Nazareth and called to Jesus that it was time to come in to supper, the name would have sounded quite ordinary. But the boy grew to manhood, and did marvellous things. He spoke in a fashion that had never before been heard. There was an authority in his voice that made even thoughtless people listen. There was a miraculous power in his hands that could make sick people well. There was such majesty in his bearing, that even when hanging helpless on a Cross, his dignity could not be destroyed. And in the end, it proved that he was stronger than death itself, and on the first Easter morning he came out of the dark tomb like a conqueror. And then men realised that Jesus the carpenter of Nazareth was none other than Jesus Christ, Son of the living God, who had come to bring deliverance to us sinners in the world. 'Jesus' means 'God saves'. And in this Man, crucified, risen, Lord of life and death, they could indeed see and feel the saving power of God.

We sometimes forget that the Christian Faith is centred in a Person. True beliefs, religious observances, integrity of character, loyalty to moral standards—all these are important. All these are involved in any true living of the Christian life. But they are not the central thing. The central thing is devotion to a Person, trust in a Person, obedience to a Person: Jesus.

> *How sweet the name of Jesus sounds*
> *In a believer's ear.*
> *It soothes his sorrows, heals his wounds,*
> *And drives away his fear.*

It is no accident that all the greatest and most beloved hymns are hymns that recall Jesus: his matchless life of love and courage, his sympathy, his sufferings, his death, his resurrection.

When a Christian congregation bow their heads in prayer, they offer every prayer in the name of Jesus Christ. He is our Great Intercessor. It is because of his forgiving love that we dare to bring our needs to God.

When we preachers go up into the pulpit, our chief task, our marvellous privilege, is to preach Jesus. If ever we forget that, then our sermons become superficial. They lose spiritual warmth and vitality. They lose appeal. Because it is Jesus who alone can satisfy the deepest needs of men and women: the need for comfort, for counsel, for forgiveness, for assurance.

Once, some strangers from another country came up to Andrew and said: "Sir, we wish to see Jesus. Can you help us to find our way to Jesus?" That is the deepest need of every man and woman: to be brought into touch with Jesus. Yes, and before we look for him, he is waiting to welcome and bless us; reaching out towards us: in the Holy Scriptures, in the fellowship of the Church, in Baptism, in Holy Communion. "Let the children come to me." "I am the Bread of life; whoever comes to me shall never be hungry."

Jesus is himself the Gospel, the Good News. "If anyone is thirsty let him come to me." "Come to me, all whose work is hard, whose load is heavy." "I am the Light of the world." "I am the Door." "I am the Good Shepherd." "I am the Living Bread." "I am the Way, the Truth and the Life."

Jesus: "There is no other name . . . granted to men by which we may receive salvation."

His enemies had that name crudely emblazoned on a placard and fastened it above his head as he hung on the Cross. They intended it as a slogan of mockery: "Jesus of Nazareth, King of the Jews." But it has become a slogan of triumph: "Jesus of Nazareth, King of the Jews, King of the World, Saviour of Mankind."

Today across the globe, in countless tongues and in countless places of worship, men and women turn in thought towards that Cross on a hill-top, and pronounce in reverence, in humility, in penitence, in hope, in devotion, that name by which we may be saved: JESUS.

It is almost the first word we learnt as children when our mother taught us to fold our hands in prayer. It is the best word that we can have on our lips when we come to die.

The old-fashioned evangelicals were right when thy spoke of "coming to Christ" as the vitally important thing, the beginning of the Christian life. When you read the biographies of those whom we call 'saints', you notice that the distinguishing thing about them was their devotion to Jesus, their sense of his nearness and kindness, and their practice of turning continually to him for guidance and strength and peace of mind.

Perhaps you ask: "Where do I most easily meet with Jesus and get this sense of his Presence?"

Well, for one thing, we meet him in the Bible. It is there that we get our first and supreme understanding of him. Because in its pages, we find the story of that strange, matchless life, of that "ministry of love, a whirlwind three years in which he spent himself to secure the good of mankind," as H. W. Montefiore has described it. As we watch him, that Man of Galilee "going about doing good", laying his healing hands on the sick, offering his friendship to the lonely, the unwanted, the despised, offering his forgiveness to those who had made a mess of their lives, bringing new hope to those who had lost heart, talking to unimportant people; as we listen to his words, sometimes comforting and reassuring, sometimes stabbing and frightening, but always charged with a sense of authority and moral power heard in no other voice; above all as we see him hanging on a Cross, lifted high in helpless agony, while the careless crowds go by, and hearing him praying, praying for his torturers—something extraordinary happens.

We realise that all this is not simply a chapter out of an ancient history book, the story of a Person who lived and died 1900 years ago, but that in some strange fashion "that Person bursts through the records"; that he is our contemporary, and not ours only, but the eternal contemporary of Everyman of every age and condition. That he is looking at *me*, speaking to *me*, judging *me*, offering forgiveness and healing and friendship to *me*. That on the Cross he prayed for *me*. That when I see him with the light of Easter morning in his eyes, it is my name he speaks.

That is why the Bible is a unique book; because in its pages we meet Jesus, "the same yesterday and today". That is why the Bible is the world's best seller. Not because it is fine literature, not because it contains most interesting chapters of ancient history, not even because it provides profound wisdom on the meaning and conduct of human life. But because, when we open it, we are confronted by a "living Figure who breaks through the printed pages of the Gospels" and speaks to us and draws us irresistibly to himself.

We meet this same Living Figure in the Church. The Church is his family. He founded it. He rules it. He loves it. He gave himself for it. He guides it. He watches over it. He works through it. He is close to it.

Jesus said: "Wherever two or three have met together in my name, I am there among them." It is that promise which draws us Sunday by Sunday to our services for corporate worship. We know that as together we bow our heads in prayer or lift our voices in praise or listen to the reading from the book, he the Master, our Unseen Friend, is amongst us. And perhaps above all, that sense of his nearness, his Presence, becomes vivid in that observance which he himself gave us, the Lord's Supper or Holy Communion. "Here, O my Lord, I see thee face to face" we sing in the familiar hymn. And, however dimly, each one of us knows something of that experience. At his own Table, he meets with us, he greets us, he accepts us, unworthy; he looks upon us with kindness and mercy, he gives himself to us: "This is my Body, which is broken for you." "This Cup is the new covenant in my blood, shed for many for remission of sins."

Wherever a Christian congregation is strong and vital and effective, it is because the strong living Presence of Christ is among his people.

But, on our side, is there nothing we must do?

Yes, in the Christian life, the doing is the response to the Master's offer.

"Come," says Jesus, "Ask, Seek, Knock, Take, Receive." It means humility; which is the chief thing Jesus wants of us, and the last thing that many of us are willing to give. Because when we seek, knock, ask, come, we acknowledge our own spiritual poverty and our need of him.

It means also self-committal. Because when we come and ask and take and receive his gifts, then we commit ourselves to be his people, his disciples, his followers, his friends—to our lives' end.

So, we go from his Table, his holy place, back into the world, committed to do the Master's will.

THE CLOSED CIRCLE BROKEN

A Christmas Sermon

"I have good news for you: there is great joy coming to the whole people. Today in the city of David a deliverer has been born to you—the Messiah, the Lord."

St. Luke 2: 10-11

"He shall be called Emmanuel, a name which means 'God is with us'."

St. Matthew 1: 23

Christmas Day! And all round the world people are gathered in imagination and prayer and worship at the door of the stable at Bethlehem, to listen once again to the matchless story of the first Christmas night, of the angels' song, and the shepherds, and the Child who was laid in a manger for his cradle. Once again we have lighted the candles on the Christmas tree, exchanged greetings and cards, and look forward to parties and family festivities. And of course it is all beautiful and proper and good.

Yet we need to beware lest when we have so invested Christmas with the magic of symbolism and the beauty of carols and nostalgic memories of childhood, we may come to think of it as a scene in an ancient fairy-tale, having no roots in the real world.

On the contrary, the birth of Jesus Christ happened in history. "Unto you is born this day, in the city of David, a Saviour." The life of Jesus of Nazareth, that is to say, is not simply a lovely legend like one of the old Greek myths, or Icelandic sagas, or one of our own Celtic tales. It is plain, hard fact. It happened at a certain specific moment in history, in a certain small Eastern country. Both Matthew and Luke are very particular to date this birthday as exactly as possible. Jesus was born here on our earth, in the little provincial town of Bethlehem—a town of no special significance or importance, like Kirkintilloch, or Kilmarnock. Born of humble parents, his childhood spent in a simple home, at Nazareth; a home where hard work and simple fare were taken for granted. His whole life was spent among the towns and villages and fields of that small land. Bethlehem, Nazareth, Capernaum, Jericho, Jerusalem, and many nameless villages: that was the setting of the Life that began on the first Christmas Day; a Life lived in our ordinary world.

So that the Christmas proclamation is firmly rooted in history. That unique life was woven into the common warp and woof of our homespun human lot. The little Child born that first Christmas night came into exactly the same sort of world as any of the babies born in Britain last night: a world of work and danger, of suffering and happiness, of laughter and tears, of love and hate, of loneliness and comradeship; a world full of poverty and prostitution, and war, and fear, and death.

The birth of Jesus of Nazareth gave new meaning to history. There is a creed which has become curiously fashionable in many quarters in recent decades. One might call it the Creed of the Closed Circle.

The scientist perhaps inevitably usually works within this closed circle philosophy. To the majority of those influenced by the scientific outlook this universe is like a great complex machine, determined by certain unalterable physical and biological laws. Human life and history, like the life and history of all other living creatures, are subject to these mechanical laws. So long as he works within these limiting conditions, Man can do wonderful things. He can adapt the forces of Nature to his own purposes. He can explore and experiment; he can make and destroy. He can plan society in accordance with his desires, and then periodically smash up the whole system of civilisation which he has so laboriously built up. But one thing he cannot do. He cannot escape from the circle.

The politician works also within the narrow limits of this same philosophy. The weakness in so much of our social and industrial planning, our political programmes and our international diplomacy, is that they too are conducted, as it were, within a closed circle, a closed circle which also seems often a vicious circle. Hence the somewhat cynical view taken by so many engaged in public affairs. "History only repeats itself," they say. "Progress is an illusion. You need not expect the world to get better, for it moves only in an endless cycle. You need not expect men to change, for they only act true to type. Being finite and fallible they always have and always will make mistakes, commit blunders and follies, involve themselves in pain and trouble. There have always been class struggles, national wars, racial conflicts. This is inevitable and can be expected to continue."

We men, that is to say, according to this creed are shut up as it were inside a great closed circle; with our sins and sufferings, our cleverness and conceit, our nuclear submarines and hydrogen bombs. The one thing that cannot happen is that man should break through the closed circle into real freedom, or that anyone or anything from outside should break into the circle and so infringe the unalterable laws of Nature.

On this view, of course, all history is simply an endless cycle of events without purpose or meaning. Now Christmas is a complete repudiation of this closed circle creed. It proclaims that Man is not shut up in an endless cycle of mechanical happenings. It proclaims that Man is not left alone with his own moral and intellectual powers, to plan and labour and succeed or fail, as best he may. It proclaims that Man is not left alone with his own sins and sufferings, to blunder and suffer and endure, and endure and suffer and blunder again and again, world without end. On the contrary, says the Christmas message, above and over-arching all human affairs there is a God, and a God, moreover, who has actually broken into the closed circle in his own son Jesus Christ.

That birth at Bethlehem which we celebrate every Christmas was not simply one among the thousands of births which are registered every year. It was a unique event which threw a new light upon all other events. It marked the beginning of a new era in human history. We re-date the whole calendar from the day of that birth in a stable.

Why? Because God had broken into the closed circle. "The Word became flesh; he came to dwell among us." Or, as St. Luke puts it, "Today in the city of David a deliverer has been born to you—the Messiah, the Lord." That is to say, into this apparently closed world of human struggle and folly and sin, God sent his own Son: to dwell among us, to share the pain and laughter and tears of men, to experience in his own person disappointment, loneliness, hope, fear, and all the other testing vicissitudes of our human lot.

Now, if the Christmas Story is true, then it gives us the clue to the interpretation of all history. History becomes no longer a blind cycle of meaningless happenings, but the setting in which God's purpose of love and redemption is being worked out. The fatal fallacy of the closed circle creed is that it leaves God out of account. It forgets that what is impossible to men is possible to God. It forgets that the final issues in human affairs are not with the dictators nor yet the democracies, but in the almighty hands of One whose name is Love.

For the force which broke into the closed circle of human history was not the force of tyranny or arbitrary despotism, but the power of creative, redemptive love. In Jesus Christ we see God's Son in human flesh, and living on earth among men, and by his mighty love not only sharing in, but overcoming all the forces of evil and frustration and pain which we men and women have to meet. Nothing less than that is the meaning of the Life that began at Bethlehem on the first Christmas morning.

> *Once in Royal David's city*
> *Stood a lowly cattle shed,*
> *Where a Mother laid her Baby*
> *In a manger for his bed.*
> *Mary was that mother mild,*
> *Jesus Christ her little child.*
>
> *He came down to earth from heaven*
> *Who is God and Lord of all,*
> *And his shelter was a stable,*
> *And his cradle was a stall.*
> *With the poor and mean and lowly*
> *Lived on earth our Saviour holy.*

No wonder the angel sang, "I have good news for you: there is great joy coming to the whole people." It is those good tidings which ring out like the sound of bells all through the pages of the New Testament.

The American philosopher, A. N. Whitehead, says:

"The life of Christ has the decisiveness of a supreme ideal, and that is why the history of the world divides at this point of time."

That is true, but I don't think it is an adequate statement. The life of Christ, begun at Bethlehem, did indeed set an ideal standard which is a constant challenge to mankind. But it meant much more than that. It meant the redemption of history. It meant the coming of a new, Divine power into the lives of men and women.

And the power from above which broke through, which reached down into history to reveal itself, was the power of Love:

> *Love came down at Christmas,*
> *Love all lovely, Love Divine.*
> *Love came down at Christmas,*
> *Stars and Angels gave the sign.*

John Wesley says in his *Journal*:

"I see now that if God's Love can reach up to every star and down to every poor soul on earth, it must be vastly simple."

It was vastly simple when it showed itself that first Christmas, for it came in uttermost simplicity in the form of a little child. And the coming of that Love Divine changed the whole situation.

During the war, just after a very severe air-raid on the East End of London, the King ordered his car and drove slowly through the most damaged streets. The poor, shoddy little houses had collapsed like matchwood. The women and children were terrified, the men bitter and resentful. But as the royal car passed among them and they saw the King's anxious, sad face, the whole attitude and atmosphere changed. The King was with them, his people, in it all. He would look after them. His concern and presence had somehow transformed the whole situation.

So, if one may compare Divine with human things, in an infinitely profounder sense did the coming of Christ, God's own Son, into our sin-stained, fear-haunted, suffering world transform the whole situation. We who have seen his glory in the face of a little child, who have felt the touch of that Love Divine in our own lives and seen it at work in the lives of others —discover a new grandeur in history. It is no longer sordid and futile. Through it all runs a great purpose. Behind it all, a Divine Design is being worked out, a design of love.

The life of Jesus Christ, if it proves anything, proves that love is the strongest force in the universe, stronger than hatred or cruelty, stronger than any mechanised armies or fleets of warships. The great Roman Empire, with all the proud legions of Caesar to defend it, has gone. The Kingdom of Jesus Christ, founded and guarded by love alone, is pushing its frontiers ever further and further afield.

Love is the only really creative, redemptive force, and therefore the only quality capable of saving human society. Hatred destroys, love creates. Hatred embitters, love sweetens. Hatred separates, love unites. Not long ago I had a letter from a very able woman at present in hospital. She writes:

"My prayer for all of us at this season is that we may be given courage to face the truth, endurance to go on seeking the truth, and a dynamic love to overcome the evils which threaten to bring our civilisation to chaos."

What wisdom there is in that last sentence—"dynamic love to overcome evil." We hear a great deal today about the deadly threat to human life and civilisation presented by the atomic bomb. And some people foolishly assume that the future lies with the nation which has the largest secret store of diabolic weapons in its armoury. Have we not yet learnt the lesson of Bethlehem? "The race is not to the swift nor the battle to the strong." "To shame what is strong, God has chosen what the world counts weakness," says St. Paul. Despite all temporary appearances, the future lies with the followers of him who was born in a stable: the simple people, the humble in heart, and those who rely only on the strange, mysterious power of love.

This is the real inner meaning of Christmas.

LIVING IN THE LIGHT OF THE RESURRECTION

An Easter Sermon

"O grave, where is your victory? O Death, where is your sting? . . . But, God be praised, he gives us the victory through our Lord Jesus Christ."

1 Corinthians 15: 55-57

"Jesus said, 'I am the resurrection and I am life. If a man has faith in me, even though he die, he shall come to life; and no one who is alive and has faith shall ever die. Do you believe this?' "

St. John 11: 25-26

Even the most cursory reading of the New Testament makes one thing plain: the central conviction in the faith of the first Christians was the resurrection, the victory of their Master over what seemed the invincible enemy, death.

They treasured the wonderful sayings of Jesus, so full of penetrating wisdom and incomparable comfort. They cherished countless memories of his marvellous acts of healing and help as "he went about doing good". They took pleasure in thinking about his love of children, his sympathy with the poor and the oppressed, his courage in face of danger or unpopularity. But in a sense all these things were secondary. What was central and dominating was the incredible fact that he had faced death and let it do its uttermost, had actually lain in the tomb, and then on the third day come back alive, victorious.

It was this stupendous fact, incredible yet true, that was the central thing in the faith of the first Christian believers and the central thing in the preaching of the first Christian evangelists. That was the distinctive thing about the Gospel: it was Good News because it proclaimed Christ Jesus crucified, risen, and alive for evermore, and because it proclaimed that the man who accepts and holds to Christ shares in this victory over death. "Christ was raised to life—the first fruits of the harvest of the dead . . . As in Adam all men die, so in Christ all will be brought to life."

It is this belief in the resurrection, moreover, which makes the writings of the New Testament so resonant with optimism and happiness. It is not that the writers are guilty of 'wishful thinking' or are unrealistic. Far from it. They write out of a situation in which they themselves were often in extreme danger; a situation in which the future of the little Christian community must have appeared, humanly speaking, full of insecurity and peril. They were only too well aware of the terrible forces of evil rampant in the world. They knew the tragic reality of both sin and suffering in the lives of men and women.

Yet in spite of all that, the New Testament writings ring with the note of hope and confidence and joy. And the source of that hope and joy and confidence is the resurrection of Jesus Christ and the marvellous new vistas which it opens up. Here were people who felt that they had gained a new mastery over life. Nothing could any longer terrify them or plunge them into despair.

"O grave, where is your victory? O Death, where is your sting? . . . But, God be praised, he gives us the victory through our Lord Jesus Christ."

They were living in the light of the resurrection. And in that light the whole universe had been transformed. Evil, danger, suffering, work, friendship, life, death: everything had taken on a new look.

Are we twentieth-century Christians living in the light of the resurrection? Is life for us illuminated by its splendour? Is our whole outlook shot through with confidence and joy? Dr. L. P. Jacks wrote in one of his books about "the lost radiance" of Christianity. If there is truth in that phrase, I believe it is that many of us even in the Church have weakened in our grasp of this central truth of the Gospel: that by his resurrection Christ has "brought life and immortality to light" and given us the mastery.

What then does it mean to live in the light of the resurrection?

It means living as people who are already here and now in touch with the eternal world. So many people live as though this visible tangible physical world were all, and as though their whole span of life were just the sixty or seventy or eighty years of this earthly existence. They concern themselves only with material things, at least subconsciously; they are haunted by the thought of the passing of the years and the brevity of life. They are determined to get the utmost possible of happiness and wealth and success in the short time that belongs to them. But in their very search for happiness, in their very haste to be rich, and in their very longing for honour and fame, there is something feverish and restless. And underneath all their work and their fun, all their activities and ambitions, there is a hidden sense of dissatisfaction, disappointment, and frustration. Within the narrow limits of this short earthly life, they feel cabined and confined. It is good, but it is not enough.

But when we grasp the stupendous truth of the resurrection we know that this visible world of earth and time is not all but that we are already here and now in touch with the eternal world. Dr. Jowett tells of a shoemaker whom he used sometimes to visit in a seaside town. The man worked in a very small room looking on to the street. One day Dr. Jowett asked him if he didn't feel rather oppressed by the smallness of the room. "Oh no," he said, "because when the room seems too narrow, I just open this door." And he threw open a door at the back of the shop, and suddenly one looked out on to a far-stretching vista of sea and sky.

So Christ, by his resurrection, has opened a door by which we are brought into touch with a new world. We are no longer cabined and confined. We find ourselves looking out to infinite horizons. Our whole life has been given new dimensions. We are no longer haunted by the thought of the swift passing of the years, because Christ has brought life and immortality to light.

This new kind of life is not something which belongs to the future. It is already within our grasp. "The risen life begins now." And when, for any one of us, it does begin, then we see everything from a new perspective. Our work is still as impor-tant as ever, but we no longer work feverishly; and when the time comes to lay it down, we no longer feel frustrated or cheated. We still enjoy the comfort and pleasure of material possessions, but we do not set too great a value on them, nor strive too passionately for them; because we know that spiritual goods are both more precious and more lasting, and that our true treasure is in heaven "where neither moth nor rust can corrupt." We are still called to play our part as good citizens of the community in which we live on earth, and to do everything we can for its welfare; but always to remember to keep our faces set towards that "city which has foundations, whose builder and maker is God."

We shall still love the dear familiar beauties of earth: the yellow daffodils standing up tall and straight among the grass on a spring morning; the snow-covered hills shining in the winter sunlight; a gaggle of geese on the wing passing overhead against a sunset sky; or the vast Atlantic rollers sweeping in and up a spacious beach. We shall still love these beauties of earth; but when the time comes to leave them, we shall know that God has even more wonderful beauties to show us "beyond this bourne of space and time."

We shall still dread suffering and pain, for ourselves and for others. But even through it, hope will gleam, because we know "that our troubles are slight and short-lived; and their outcome an eternal glory which outweighs them far"; and that "the sufferings we now endure bear no comparison with the splendour as yet unrevealed, which is in store for us."

That is what it means to live in the light of the resurrection; it gives us new and wider horizons.

We know that this earthly life, for all its fascination and interest and possibility is no more than a first phase, as it were a prelude to the infinitely more wonderful phases of existence that are to follow. Death is formidable because it marks a great change; testing because it is a passing from the familiar to the unknown. Formidable but not fearsome. Testing but not tragic.

Our thoughts and hopes and aspirations are not bounded by the narrow confines of three score years and ten. For Christ by his resurrection has shown us infinite horizons. He has set us free from time, and told us to live as those who are made to inherit eternity. If then some of our present plans come to nothing, if some of our endeavours seem to meet with frustration, we oughtn't to grieve too much.

An over-busy schoolmistress used to say: "I never have time to paint nowadays. But I console myself by remembering that I shall have plenty of time in heaven to paint and to do all the other things I specially want." D. M. Macgregor says:

K

"If you and I have only a few years to dispose of, we are justified in refusing adventures. Like ancient shipmen, we should continuously make our way from headland to headland, keeping close to the things we see. But if a greater life is ours, we need not fear to launch out into the deep, engaging in tasks in which we are bound to fail, and cherishing hopes which cannot possibly be satisfied within the narrow bounds of earth and time."

If Time takes some things away from us, yet we know that the best things cannot be taken away. "There are three things that last for ever: faith, hope, and love," says St. Paul.

And finally, if we live in the light of the resurrection, although we shall still shrink perhaps from the thought of death, alike for ourselves and for those we love best, yet even the thought of death will be swallowed up in victory. How utterly different is a Christian death-bed from a pagan death-bed!

In a famous passage John Bunyan describes the passing of Mr. Valiant for Truth:

"'I am going to my Father's,' he said; "and though with great difficulty I have got thither, yet now I do not repent me of all the troubles I have been at to arrive where I am. My sword I give to him that shall succeed me in my pilgrimage, and my courage and skill to him that can get it. My marks and scars I carry with me to be a witness for me that I have fought his battles who will now be my rewarder.'

"When the day that he must go hence was come, many accompanied him to the river-side, into which as he went he said, 'Death, where is thy sting?' and as he went down deeper, he said, 'Grave, where is thy victory?' So he passed over, and all the trumpets sounded for him on the other side."

CHRIST AND THE CHURCH

". . . and appointed him (Christ) as supreme head to the church . . ."

Ephesians 1: 22

"Christ loved the church and gave himself up for it."

Ephesians 5: 25

"I was caught up by the Spirit; and behind me I heard a loud voice, like the sound of a trumpet . . . And when I turned I saw seven standing lamps of gold, and among the lamps one like a son of man."

Revelation 1: 10, 12, 13

When this strange book of Revelation was written, the Church of the first century had been passing through days of dire and determined persecution. One after another the Roman emperors had resolved to extinguish this new faith. Governors of the various provinces had received orders to deal pitilessly with those who refused to worship Caesar. The men and women who professed and called themselves Christians were persecuted in countless ways. Often they were exiled from their homes and friends; many suffered torture and death. "I saw underneath the altar the souls of those who had been slaughtered for God's Word."

A favourite punishment was exile, especially to the quarries and mines. The writer of this mysterious and wonderful book of Revelation was one of those who had been thus banished. He had been sent to the small island called Patmos lying off the coast about fifteen miles from Ephesus. And there in his loneliness he had time to meditate on many things; above all on the state of the churches, the persecuted churches in Asia Minor which he knew and loved: at Smyrna, Ephesus, Pergamos and Troas, in Laodicea, Hierapolis, Thyatira, and Sardis, in Philadelphia and Colossae. He knew how many of them were haunted by terror, tempted to compromise, or to give up their religion altogether. I suppose as he thought of them—how weak they were, how young in the faith, among them not many noble, not many wise, not many mighty—he must have wondered, would they be able to endure, to survive through those stormy days of persecution without and fears within; or would the Christian Faith perhaps, for all its splendour, be extinguished by the forces of darkness?

And then, on a certain Sunday, there was given to John a remarkable vision. He "saw seven standing lamps of gold, and among the lamps one like a son of man, robed down to his feet, with a golden girdle round his breast; . . . his eyes flamed like fire, . . . his voice was like the sound of rushing waters, . . . and his face shone like the sun in full strength." What did it mean? The seven golden candlesticks, he realised, symbolised the seven churches. It meant that the eternal Christ, the Christ who was dead and is alive again, the Christ victorious, mighty in his power, unfailing in his love, would be with his Church and his own people for ever, holding them safe in his own hand, guiding them, strengthening them, protecting them.

That is what the outside world can never understand. It thinks of the Church simply as a human institution, and it wonders how the Church goes on, recovers from its sicknesses, rallies from its failures, survives in spite of its persecutions and sufferings.

A few years ago, during the tragic tribal disturbances in Kenya, African Christians were subjected to terrible sufferings; and many, standing true to their faith, surrendered their lives. From this ordeal the Church in Kenya has emerged stronger in faith and more united in fellowship. And today on the outskirts of Nairobi there stands a new place of worship, the Church of the Martyrs, already too small for the crowded congregations that gather there Sunday by Sunday. At the eastern end, stretching from floor to roof, they have erected a great blood-red cross; symbol of triumph through suffering and sacrifice.

The world does not realise that a Christian community has supernatural resources. The Risen Christ stands in its midst, to sustain and comfort and strengthen his people in the time of their need. Without him, it would soon dissolve into uselessness or worldliness or despair.

We sometimes almost forget that tremendous fact of Christ's sustaining Presence. Yet the New Testament writers go on reminding us of it. The great hymns all speak of it: "The Church's One Foundation is Jesus Christ her Lord." "Christ is made the Sure Foundation." "Christ the head and corner-stone." "I love thy Kingdom Lord, the House of thine above."

Whenever the life and spirit of the Church are renewed, it is because she has had a new vision of Christ and turns to him in new trust and humility, expectation and obedience.

The Christian Church is built upon belief in one transcendent fact: the fact of Christ. The Man who lived as a carpenter in Galilee, the Man who was done to death on a Cross outside the gates of Jerusalem, the Man who somehow conquered death, came back from the grave, and for almost 2000 years has been making an unparalleled impact upon history and upon the minds and hearts of tens of thousands of ordinary men and women in many lands.

It is upon this fact of Christ that the Church is built, and we who are his followers know that it is the living Presence and Power of this same Christ that sustains the Church from genera-tion to generation. The Word and the Sacraments (the two great distinctive possessions of the Church) alike point us to Christ. Through the Word he speaks to us. In the Lord's Supper he gives himself to us.

Journeying in remoter parts of our own country, it is aston-ishing to discover what long distances Ministers have sometimes to travel in order to make certain that Word and Sacrament are brought within reach of every man and woman. I think of a parish Minister in the island of Mull, who almost every Sunday drives 25 miles to hold an act of worship for a small handful of people in a distant hamlet. Why? Because he knows that those men and women are sustained by the reading and preaching of the Gospel of Christ.

It is the same with the Sacraments. From the very earliest days of Christianity, Christians have kept at the centre of their religious life the Breaking of Bread; knowing that as they gathered round the Lord's Table he himself would be there to meet them, to gladden them with the sense of his Presence, to strengthen them with his grace, to feed them with the Living Bread.

Christ with his Church. That is the supernatural fact which, amid all the ups and downs, successes and failures, persecution, indifference, danger, remains: Christ is with his Church. They are his people, called by his name, signed with his seal, nour-ished by his Sacrament; fed from his Table, edified by his Word, committed to his cause. And he is with them. He will not desert them. Even though they fail him, he will go on loving them. Though they refuse to listen, he will go on speaking to them. Though they turn away in heedlessness or rebelliousness, he will go on stretching out his hand towards them.

When entering the Cathedral Church of Copenhagen, the first object that strikes the eye of a visitor is a great statue which stands in the centre of the Eastern wall directly behind the high altar. The work of the famous sculptor, Thorwaldsen, it depicts the figure of Christ, standing in an attitude of mingled majesty and tenderness. He is leaning slightly forward, with hand outstretched as if in invitation and welcome. Underneath are engraved the words "Come unto Me." As a worshipper, kneeling at the altar rail, takes the bread and the wine of the Sacrament, it is almost as though he were receiving them directly from the hand of the Saviour himself, and heard the gracious words: "I am the Bread of life. Whoever comes to me shall never be hungry."

Christ not only sustains the Church, he uses the Church. He is "Supreme Head" and therefore can command. The Church is meant to be his instrument, to be used in the carrying out of his purposes.

When he departed from this earth, and from their visible sight, he gave his disciples one final command: "Go forth to every part of the world, and proclaim the Good News to the whole creation."

We are told that St. Andrew brought his own brother and introduced him to Jesus. There is the perennial mission of the Church: to introduce men and women to Jesus.

Hence evangelism must always be a central note in the life and work of the Church. All our plans and programmes and activities and organisations must be tested by one ultimate standard: Are they helping to introduce men and women and boys and girls to Christ, and to keep them in touch with Christ?

In other words, the Church is Christ's instrument in the world, to win the world for his Kingdom and cause.

Yet what a poor instrument it often is! In the early chapters of this book of Revelation the writer gives a brief assessment of the spiritual state of seven different churches or congregations in Asia: their achievements and their failures. Every congregation, every Church, would do well at least from time to time to make an act of self-examination, to try honestly as in God's sight to see where it is truly living up to its calling and where it is failing.

There are two serious weaknesses in the life of the Church today which spoil its usefulness as an instrument of Christ: disunity and indifference.

1. *Disunity.* We talk of The Church but in fact there are many churches; each 'thirled' to its own customs and traditions, each flaunting its own denominational label, each issuing its own pronouncements, each making its separate plans and policy.

Thank God, in our own time a change of outlook is gradually taking place. Christians of long-divided denominations are beginning to listen and talk to each other, beginning to see the evil of disunity and the harm it does to the cause of Christ. We are becoming a little more humble; a little more ready to believe that we have something to learn from others, with their different traditions and customs. Even the centuries-old barbed-wire barrier between Roman Catholic and Protestant has recently been lowered a little, and a new spirit of charity is transforming the atmosphere.

That enterprise with the somewhat formidable name, the Ecumenical Movement, is perhaps the most significant fact in the religious life of this twentieth century. Gradually it is drawing members of many different Christian traditions into a new spirit of fellowship and a new willingness to understand one another.

2. *Indifference.* The words addressed to the church at Laodicea are sad words: "I know all your ways; you are neither hot nor cold. How I wish you were either hot or cold! . . . All whom I love, I reprove and discipline; Be on your metal therefore and repent."

Isn't that a word to our own church in Scotland today? Going up and down the country one sees little sign of hostility to the Christian cause. But there is much spiritual indifference. Some in every congregation are enthusiastic in Christ's cause, ready to use their gifts in his service, eager to forward his Kingdom. But there are still too many who do little, who give little, who care little. Many who like to have their names on the Communicants' Roll, but only appear occasionally in God's House on God's Day.

Some people think of the Church as a kind of pleasant social club, to which they can give as much or as little time and attention as they choose. Some people think of it as a kind of spiritual clinic which provides help for the discouraged and over-burdened, the sad and the puzzled.

But when you open the New Testament you see that the Church is actually quite different. It is an army, engaged on a great campaign, in the service of a great cause; its members expected to be ready for hardship, effort, danger, as good soldiers of Jesus Christ. And that army will win, and we his followers are called to share in its battles and in its victory.

There are many pessimists in the world of our time. But in face of all pessimism and despair, the Christian bells ring out their joyful proclamation. Let us keep constantly before us the assurance that the risen, victorious Christ is with his Church; the Christ who in his own person conquered evil and pain and death itself, and is alive for evermore. It is that faith in a risen Saviour and Lord which makes the whole New Testament resound with a note of triumph. The forces of the world, the forces of unbelief and materialism and earthly pride, are strong; but in the end victory is certain for the army of God. The Church is no man-made human society, it is a supernatural society. Its power is not due to its wealth or its social prestige, to the efficiency of its organisation, the cleverness of its planners, the brilliance of its preachers; but to the presence of the risen Christ. Although in this world, it is yet not of this world. Its power is from above. It has resources of which the world knows nothing. There lies our help and confidence for the future. That is why, as T. S. Eliot says:

"It goes up and up in the sky, and on and on through the years, and it speaks with its lights and its bells, in the night and in the sunshine. And it stands when you and I are dust, all through the years, going on for ever and ever."

THE HOLY COMMUNION

"And he took bread, gave thanks, and broke it; and he gave it to them, with the words: 'This is my body'."

St. Luke 22: 19

If the question were asked by an outsider, "What is the most distinctive observance of the Christian Church?" almost inevitably the answer would be: "Christians meet together for the observance of an ancient rite which they call variously the Lord's Supper, the Holy Communion, or the Eucharist."

The sacrament of the Lord's Supper or Eucharist is the great central religious observance of the Christian Church. It is observed in every part of the world where the name of Jesus Christ is honoured. It has been kept from the very earliest days. It is the supreme act of Christian worship. It is the supreme comfort of the Christian life. It goes back to the most primitive period of Christian history—before any accepted forms of worship had been prepared, any creed formulated, any special buildings erected. In those earliest days we are, however, told that Christians "continued steadfastly in the Apostles' teaching and in fellowship and in breaking of bread and in prayers."

All this becomes understandable when we remember that this Sacrament was instituted by Christ himself. It is not simply a fine piece of ceremonial calculated to appeal to the eye and ear. Not a piece of moving symbolism calculated to touch the emotions. Not simply an act of ecclesiastical drama designed to induce vague mystical feelings. The Lord's Supper is rooted in history. It goes back, and carries us back in imagination, to a particular place, and a particular day and hour. The sacrificial death which it symbolically proclaims actually happened. On the evening before that death the Master, meeting alone with his disciples in the quiet of an upstairs room, took bread, and after breaking it said, "This is my body." So the Sacrament was instituted. It was as though He said to them: "What we have done here together this evening, you are to go on doing for all time. When you do it in future, you will no longer be able to see me with your mortal eyes. But it will always be my feast and I shall be with you at the Table."

The first friends and followers of Jesus obeyed that injunction. On the first day of each week they came together for prayer and worship and the breaking of bread. The friends and followers of Jesus have continued, generation after generation, obeying his command.

With the gradual expansion of the Christian community, many different liturgical customs and uses have been evolved in connection with the celebration of the Lord's Supper. But behind all these differences, whether the ceremonial be simple or elaborate, whether it be a Sung Eucharist in a spacious Cathedral or a homely service in some small village church—always the central things, the principal words, the significant ritual actions are the same. And always on the Holy Table, in the sight of all, are set bread and wine; bread which will be broken, wine which will be poured out. Always in receiving the bread and the wine, the worshippers plead "the one true pure immortal sacrifice".

This sacred rite which is the central act of the Church's worship is not of human invention. It was the Saviour who himself took these simple things, bread and wine, and invested them with unfading significance. People sometimes ask, "Is the Sacrament really important? Is it necessary to salvation?" Surely it is answer enough if we remember that Christ our Lord instituted it:

> *What he did, at supper seated,*
> *Christ ordained to be repeated,*
> *His memorial ne'er to cease;*
> *And, his word for guidance taking,*
> *Bread and wine we hallow, making*
> *Thus his sacrifice of peace.*

What does the Lord's Supper or Eucharist signify?

In spite of certain doctrinal differences among the various branches of the Church, there would probably be a large measure of agreement in answering this question.

1. THROUGH THIS SACRAMENT CHRIST SPEAKS TO US

"This is my body, given for you." The breaking of the bread, the pouring of the wine, are more eloquent than many words.

Because we know what happened to that Body. On the very next day, It was beaten, tortured, stripped, nailed to a Cross on a hillside, and left there in shame and agony to die.

Even non-Christians and pagans are shocked. "One of the most dastardly deeds of history," they say, "an innocent good-living man put savagely to death."

They are right. But we Christians know there was much more to it than that. He, the sinless One, hanging on that Cross, was voluntarily suffering for us; bearing our guilt, accepting our punishment, taking upon his own shoulders our sins, that he might set us free from sin. As Hugh Martin has said:

"The Last Supper pointed forward to the Cross. Every Lord's Supper points back to the Cross, as memorial of a life offered and broken and laid down once for all. We observe it in remembrance that Christ died for us."

2. THROUGH THE EUCHARIST CHRIST COMES TO US

Jesus gave to his disciples, and bequeathed to future generations, incomparable teaching about the living of the good life. Never have such lofty standards of truthfulness, generosity, purity, courage, obedience to God, unselfishness towards neighbours, been set before the world as are to be found alike in his words and his example. But if that were all, it would only leave men helpless and humiliated before the demands of an impossible standard. If Christianity offered only a code of moral rules, an abstract ideal of perfection to pursue, it would provide little encouragement.

But through the Sacrament he strengthens us by his own Presence and spiritual power. Within the various parts of the Church different aspects of this Sacrament have been emphasised. But upon one fact all are agreed. It is a fact of experience no less than of belief: namely that gathered at the Lord's Table, and with the sincere and humble intention to keep the feast according to his commandment, his promise is fulfilled: "Where two or three have met together in My Name, I am there among them." In the Moravian Church at the celebration of the Sacrament, it is the custom to keep a place at the Communion Table empty for Christ the Saviour, who is there; unseen, but not unknown.

In one of his novels, Neil Gunn describes a family supper in a seaside village cottage in Caithness-shire, before the elder son goes off to Australia and a daughter to service in London:

"This was more than a normal tea; more even than the evidence of a mother's kindness. She broke oatcakes for them and cut bread. She filled their cups. She watched each one and helped him to the elements on the table. She smiled. Her heart was full of love and broke itself amongst them . . . The paraffin lamp shed down its soft light upon them. Their mother's body swayed in its chair, and her hands moved among the cups and poured the tea and offered to each one. Her brow was wide and calm and her dark straight hair was combed from the middle to either side."

So, if one dare compare heavenly with earthly things, at his own Table Christ is present. He meets with us; he speaks to us, he feeds us, he gives himself to us, he draws us more closely and intimately to himself than at any other time or place in our earthly life.

The Bishop of Singapore, imprisoned by the Japanese, tells how during a time when he was being constantly tortured and maltreated, he was yet able to celebrate Holy Communion each morning, and by the Sacrament was marvellously strengthened to endure.

3. THROUGH THE EUCHARIST CHRIST SUMMONS US HIS FOLLOWERS TO COSTLY SERVICE

We are frequently tempted to shut our eyes to this aspect of Christianity, pretending to ourselves that to be a follower of Jesus and a member of his Church does not really involve us in any necessary self-denial or sacrifice. But if we are honest we know that that is not true. Open the New Testament almost anywhere, and there it is—the inescapable Cross at the centre of Christ's teaching, at the centre of his life, at the centre of the lives of his disciples. "If anyone wishes to be a follower of mine, he must leave self behind; day after day he must take up his cross, and come with me." The broken bread of the Sacrament reminds us of that hard truth.

We do wrong if we think of the Lord's Supper as simply a means towards personal sanctification: or a kind of spiritual comfort to be hugged to our own souls, least of all as a sort of escape from the harsh realities of life into a secluded region of mystical peace and devotion. On the contrary, the Sacrament reaches out in its message and its challenge from the sanctuary into the world, from the holy place into all the common places of ordinary life.

It is significant that Christ should have used, for this supreme act in the worship of the Christian Church, the simplest of all commodities, bread. Bread: the staple diet of every family in the land. Bread: that for which all men work at their different trades, and professions; so that the head of the household, going out to his daily labour, is called 'the breadwinner'. Bread: of which even the prisoner in a concentration camp is given his ration. Bread: of which, on a bitter day of frost and snow, even the little birds that come to the window-sill can count on their crumbs. Bread: the very symbol of human need and human toil.

You see what it means: that simple Thing lying consecrated on the Holy Table. It is a summons: a summons to use all bread to God's glory; to try and fulfil God's purposes and do his will in all our bread-making and bread-winning and bread-distributing. "A civilisation," Dr. L. P. Jacks once said, "saves its soul by the way it wins its daily bread."

Broken Bread: with what silent challenge it speaks to us! For he who sat at the Table with his disciples went out from the peace and the friendship and the quiet candle-light of the upper room back into the tumult and hazards and sins and needs of the world, allowing his Body to be broken on a Cross, "for us men and our salvation". Those first-century disciples went out to make their sacrifice in a cruel dangerous world. And so, as we take into our hands the broken bread of the Sacrament it calls us also to self-forgetting and sacrificial service in his world. For, as has been rightly said, "Life only becomes fruitful when it becomes sacrificial." And "the action of the Eucharist is always the action of Christ Himself, perpetually offering himself for the life of the world." We, his followers, are called to identify ourselves with his Divine self-offering.

MARY, THE MOTHER OF JESUS

"Mary treasured up all these things and pondered over them."

St. Luke 2: 19

"Then Jesus went back with them (his parents) to Nazareth, and continued to be under their authority; his mother treasured up all these things in her heart."

St. Luke 2: 51

In large parts of Christendom, and from very early times, Mary the mother of Christ has been accorded a deep and affectionate veneration and homage. In more recent times, it is true, theological dogmas regarding her person and power have been built on very frail foundations, and devotional practices have been encouraged which cannot easily find justification in Holy Scripture, and can all too easily distract attention from Christ our Lord himself, so leading to a false perspective. But on the other hand, it is to be regretted that in reaction to the possible dangers of Mariolatry, the Reformed Churches have deliberately diverted their attention from that pure, gentle and unselfish figure who moved so quietly behind the scenes in the earthly life of Jesus and across the pages of the Gospels, and who was chosen to be the unique instrument in God's purpose of redemption.

The Gospels tells us very much less than we should like to know about the childhood and early years of Jesus. Simply the two incomparable stories about his birth, and then one small but significant incident when he was twelve years old.

Even from the scattered hints and fragments of information which are given us, however, we can be certain that the supreme influence in the childhood and youth of the boy Jesus was the influence of his mother. It must have been from her that he learnt his first prayers; from her lips that he first heard the great stories of Jacob and Joseph, Samuel and Gideon, David and Saul, the passionate tones of the prophets, the moving voices of the psalmists which in later years were to be his continual comfort and inspiration. From her (speaking in utmost reverence) it must have been that he took his first impressions of life and the world of men and things.

We know little of the external life of Mary during those years in Nazareth while the family were growing up. But we can be certain that Jesus as a small boy would be constantly close to her as she did her household tasks: cooking, baking, mending, washing. It is surely those childhood memories that echo through many of his parables: the woman patching the torn piece of cloth, the woman searching for a lost silver coin, the housewife preparing the yeast for putting into the bread. All of these, almost certainly, memories of the home at Nazareth. And watching and learning from her, the boy Jesus perhaps realised that in her he saw a picture of the ideal wife and mother so movingly described in the book of Proverbs:

"She riseth also while it is yet night and giveth meat to her household. She girdeth her loins with strength and strengtheneth her arm. She layeth her hands to the spindle, and her hands hold the distaff. She stretcheth out her hands to the poor, yea, she reacheth forth her hands to the needy. She openeth her mouth with wisdom and in her tongue is the law of kindness. She looketh well to the ways of her household, and eateth not the bread of idleness. Her children arise up and call her blessed. Her husband also and he praiseth her."

While all too little is known of the outward events of Mary's life, we can yet unmistakably discern certain qualities which shine out from the Gospel page, and which have made her so loved and honoured by countless multitudes in succeeding generations.

There is her modesty. She never pushes herself forward. When the supreme experiences come to her, the birth of her Divine Son and the watching of him as he grows up, through childhood and boyhood, "in wisdom and in favour with God and men", we are simply told that "Mary treasured up all these things and pondered over them".

It is certain that she was a woman of unusual heart and spirit. For as has been said, "God does not choose his instruments at random; for his great tasks he has elect souls. He does not command coarse and careless hands to do his finest and most delicate work." And for the supreme trust ever committed to any human being, that of being the mother of the Christ, he chose this woman Mary. Yet even while conscious of the wonder of God's grace in choosing her, Mary shows an unruffled humility. To the angel who says "Greetings, most favoured one! The Lord is with you." her only response is in quiet and obedient acquiescence. "Here am I. I am the Lord's servant. As you have spoken, so be it,"

Then there is her goodness. All down the centuries, the Church and even the outside world has cherished the picture of the Virgin Mary as its picture of perfect womanhood. In her we see the lovely virtue of chastity: that virtue which the Christian ethic has always cherished and which even the most sinister and profligate secretly admire. For, to quote again the ancient book of wisdom:

"Who can find a virtuous woman, for her price is far above rubies. The heart of her husband doth safely trust in her. She will do him good and not evil all the days of her life."

Contempt for chastity, or indifference to it, is one of the greatest enemies in our social life today; poisoning the atmosphere of a home and undermining the security and dignity of marriage.

In the family at Nazareth we have a very different picture. Parenthood involves many problems and often hardships. There are some parents in our time who shirk these hardships and responsibilities. There are even women who make light of motherhood and exalt other vocations at its expense. Mary the mother of Jesus reminds us that, in spite of all its anxieties, there can be no higher vocation than looking after husband and home and sending out into the world sons and daughters who will unselfishly serve God and their fellowmen.

The Incarnation means the consecration of all motherhood. Mary represents motherhood at its purest and best. She who held in her arms as a babe the very Son of God, who taught him to speak, to fold his hands and speak his first prayer, who brought him up so simply in that humble home at Nazareth, who gave him his first ideas of the dignity and gentleness of womanhood, whose love and solicitude never failed him: is an inspiration and example of perfection to every mother to whom has been committed the gift of a child to love and care for and train.

There is another quality in Mary which I think we notice even in the few glimpses which the Gospels give of her: I mean her capacity of suffering without losing either faith or love. This, which is perhaps a special gift of womanhood, she reveals in supreme degree. Even while she stood in the temple courts with her tiny Son in her arms, the old man Simeon in prophetic vision warned her, "Indeed, a sword shall pierce through your own soul."

And this suffering came to her in later years in many ways.

There was, for example, the hour when she had to see her beloved Son leave home. How heavy is the demand made on a mother, whose very vocation is to send away from herself and out into the world those she loves best and would gladly keep by her side. With pain she bears her son, with constant care she cherishes and brings him up, and then with self-sacrificing loyalty she sends him out into the world to play his part, to do his work. Whatever her own loneliness, she must not hold him back. So it was with Mary. And again and again the best mothers, following her example, have acted in the same way. Inwardly desolate, it may be, yet bravely sending out their sons at the call of duty to some sphere of work that may take them far from home, or even into danger: to defend their country and its ideals in time of war; to colonise some distant part of the earth, to explore some tract of unknown country, to carry the Gospel of the Kingdom of God to some strange land.

Mary had to suffer also in another way. For she never perfectly understood her Divine Son. Is it to be wondered at? Do parents ever wholly understand their children? And in this case there was a barrier of mystery which disclosed itself even when he was only twelve years old, which could never be wholly broken down, which indeed was bound to become more impenetrable as the years passed. She early recognised that she could never expect wholly to understand the character of this Son who was hers, yet never quite completely hers.

In the relationship of Jesus and his mother, loving as it was, there seems always to have been, inevitably, this misunderstanding about his vocation; so that once or twice even *her* belief in him almost failed, and she tried to restrain him in his work and dissuade him from his chosen ministry.

Yet in spite of this veil which separated them, a deep and unbreakable affection bound Mary and her Son to each other.

L

Her love never failed him, any more than his failed her. Through all the long silent years at Nazareth and Capernaum he was to her the perfect son, her constant counsellor and support after Joseph's death. When he went out to his public ministry, he had to leave the home at Capernaum. His teaching and healing activities must have absorbed all his energy; but even then we may be sure his thoughts turned often with gratitude to his gentle mother. And at the end as he hung dying on a Cross, deserted even by almost all of his chosen followers and friends, Mary stood close by at the foot of that Cross; her heart broken by sorrow, torn by anguish, yet she would not leave him. And it was to her his thoughts and love instinctively turned at the end. In all the Gospels there is no scene more touching than when, in the very act of dying, Jesus commends his mother to the care of his friend John. "Jesus saw his mother, with the disciple whom he loved standing beside her. He said to her, 'Mother, there is your son'; and to the disciple, 'There is your mother'; and from that moment the disciple took her into his home."

It is little wonder that some of the greatest artists of the world have found in Mary the mother of Jesus a source of inspiration. The Reformed Churches have perhaps lost something of rare value in excluding her from their thought and love. However that may be, in her modesty, her chastity, her courage, her quiet acceptance of life's harsher experiences, she remains the ideal of womanhood and in her example every mother can find comfort and strength.

STRANGE HAPPENINGS IN A PRISON

"The jailor . . . rushed in and threw himself down before
Paul and Silas, trembling with fear. He then escorted them
out and said, 'Masters, what must I do to be saved?' "

Acts 16: 29-30

The man who blurted out that urgent desperate question had
just passed through a shattering experience.

He was the Governor of the prison in the town of Philippi.
Under his charge he had several prisoners, some perhaps
awaiting trial, some already tried and now serving their
sentence. Among them were two men whom the magistrates had
instructed him to guard with special care, as dangerous distur-
bers of the peace; their names, Paul and Silas. He had therefore had them placed in the inner cell, perhaps underground,
and to make doubly sure, had their legs made fast in the stocks.

And then, in the middle of the night, when all seemed safe
and secure, suddenly an earth tremor shook the whole building;
so that the very foundations of the gaol were rocked, the doors
flew open, the chains on the prisoners were broken. At first the
Governor, seeing the open doors, and imagining that all the
prisoners had escaped, was tempted to commit suicide. But then
through the darkness came the voice of Paul: "Do yourself no
harm. We are all here."

And at that, the gaoler called for a light, and making his
way to the cell where Paul and Silas sat in the stocks, fell down
before them and asked that desperate, urgent question:
"Masters, what must I do to be saved?"

We know nothing of the past life or character of the man.
He was a public official, entrusted with a rather difficult and
unpleasant responsibility. Probably a rough careless man, who
had taken things as they came, and given little thought to
serious matters, perhaps been a little unscrupulous in his public
and private life, with certain questionable actions at the back of
his conscience, which he didn't allow to trouble him overmuch.

But then, in a single night, he was confronted with the break-up of all the secure familiar routine of his life, with the sense of physical danger, with the possibility of losing his post as Governor, with the stark possibility of death itself. And so, in that new frame of mind, stabbed out of his complacency and security, he turns to the two strange prisoners in his charge, who seemed calm and unmoved through it all, who seemed to possess something which he lacked, and asked them: "Masters, what must I do?" What must I do, in face of the ultimate realities: insecurity, danger, death, judgment? What must I do to get my life on to a new basis? What must I do to find the secret of inner confidence and peace?

You see, the shattering experience of the earthquake had brought him to a turning-point, to a sudden crisis in his thoughtless, careless way of life.

How often that happens in the lives of men and women: the coming of some shattering experience which stabs us awake, forces us to see the true issues of life, compels us to examine ourselves honestly. It may be a crushing disaster in business; it may be the disappointment of some cherished dream or ambition; it may be the death of someone dearer to us than life itself; it may be some serious illness which suddenly snuffs out all our plans and activities and throws us into darkness and uncertainty about the future. And out of the shattering experience, with the cloak of complacency suddenly stripped from him, a man cries out: "What must I do to be saved?" Realising that he himself is a foolish, sinful being, unequal to life's emergencies, puzzled by its mysteries, frightened of its unknown terrors and possibilities, he cries out: "What must I do?"

Yet that hour of terror and despair is also the hour of hope. Because it is then that a man reaches out his hand in humility, through the darkness, to look for a hand to grasp and secure and protect him.

"What must I do?" asked the Philippian gaoler. The answer he received from Paul and Silas must certainly have seemed a curious one: "Put your trust in the Lord Jesus," they said, "and you will be saved, you and your household." But the man took it seriously; for he had realised that night that the things of ultimate importance in life were not a good salary, or a glass of beer with his friends, or even a comfortable armchair in front of the fire with his family round him. The thing of ultimate importance was to have a creed to hold on to in face of danger and earthquakes and sudden death. I suppose there and then Paul and Silas sat down and told him of the Christian Gospel, told him that there is only one Person who is Lord both of life and death; who can save us both from sin and fear. And the final picture we have is of a Baptismal Service conducted in a prison at dead of night; the gaoler and all his household, wife and children. Christians! Their pagan ways and beliefs left behind, their fears and superstitions left behind. Their sins forgiven, and they themselves committed to a new Master, Jesus Christ, and his way of life.

I have sometimes felt when paying a pastoral visit in certain homes that the husband and wife are living in a sort of shut-in world of selfish complacency and materialistic contentment. They have no interest in spiritual realities. No time for God or Church or prayer or Sacrament. They are living in imagined security. And as I come away, I feel that perhaps only some shattering experience, some piercing pain, some killing sin which shakes the house of their life to its foundations, will bring them to their senses.

We are living at a moment in history when we are all in some measure being stabbed awake and forced to face ultimate realities: the recent testings of a bomb of unimaginably destructive power sent a tremor of fear across the earth in the minds and hearts of men and women in every country. It threatens all our easy-going human security. It menaces the happiness of our homes. It threatens the safety of our children and grandchildren. It opens before us the possibility not only of personal pain and death, but of the shattering into ruin of our whole civilisation, the product of centuries of sacrifice and toil.

Silently into the minds of many people today there steals the question: "What must we do to be saved?"

And I believe that in the crisis of this mid-twentieth century, as in the town of Philippi two thousand years ago, the answer is the same: "Have faith in the Lord Jesus, and you will be saved, you and your household."

One thing is certain. With all our marvellous gadgets and gimmicks, we yet cannot save ourselves.

As an American poet puts it, in blunt modern jargon:

You will not be saved by General Motors or the prefabricated house;
You will not be saved by dialectic materialism or the Lambeth Conference;
You will not be saved by Vitamin D or the expanding universe.
In fact, you will not be saved.

There speaks the voice of the realist, who at least sees our human predicament and its peril.

But there *is* One who can save, if only we will turn to him. "Have faith in the Lord Jesus." That is the answer of the Christian Gospel. That is the answer that the Christian Church must proclaim, with all its power, to our shaken world. Christ alone can set us men free from our sins and follies and fears. Christ alone can show to the nations a better way.

TRIBULATION AND JOY

Jesus said "I have spoken thus to you, so that my joy may be in you, and your joy complete."

St. John 15: 11

Jesus said: "In the world you will have trouble."

St. John 16: 33

Christianity is full of paradoxes. We have such a paradox in this passage from St. John's Gospel. Christ is giving his last instructions and counsels to his disciples before he leaves them. He warns them of the kind of life which they must expect if they intend to follow and serve him. He tells them to be prepared for "blood and sweat and tears," for hardship and hostility. "In the world you will have trouble."

And then, almost in the same breath, he says:

"I have spoken thus to you, so that my joy may be in you, and your joy complete."

Tribulation and Joy: What a seemingly impossible contradiction! But when one examines it more closely, it is in the very conjunction of these two things that one finds the key to the Christian view of life.

In Greece in the fourth century before Christ there was a philosophical creed which for a time and in certain quarters had a great vogue. It was called Hedonism. It was based on the belief that the supreme pursuit in life ought to be the pursuit of pleasure, that as far as possible everything painful and unpleasant ought to be avoided. The sensible man was the man who realised that life is short and precarious, and who therefore seized every enjoyable experience within reach.

It seems to me that in some quarters today we are witnessing a revival of this philosophy of Hedonism: the doctrine that pleasure is the chief good. We hear a great deal about what is described as 'the right to happiness'. Not long ago someone walking down Broadway in New York noticed an enormous illuminated sign bearing the words "Life owes you an automobile"! Many people in our time imagine that life owes them what they call a good time. Meaning fun and games, parties, money, clothes. That they are somehow entitled to happiness; happiness defined in their own terms, and to be pursued at all costs, even if it means the break-up of marriage or neglect of duty or repudiation of responsibility, even if it means sometimes heartbreak for someone else.

This strange but popular creed, 'the right to happiness', receives enormous propaganda from the cinema, from the theatre, and from certain well-known and widely read sections of the Press. It is the underlying assumption of many contemporary novels. It is made the pretext for flouting many principles and standards of behaviour formerly accepted as the best signposts for right living.

But has this so-called right to happiness any real justification? *Are* we entitled to happiness? Or rather, are we sure what happiness really is? And are we setting about finding it in the proper way?

Jesus said, "In the world you shall have tribulation." He is speaking to his own followers: and he makes them no promise of pleasure, of easy living, of 'a good time'. Quite the reverse. He says, this being the kind of world it is, you must be ready for danger and difficulty, for tensions and temptations, for suffering and sorrow, even for hatred and hostility. And the more resolved you are to live the highest kind of life, the more certainly you can expect this 'tribulation'.

Here then is a creed vastly different from the philosophy of Hedonism or the 'right to happiness'. "In the world, tribulation." It is, for one thing, a far more realistic creed. To accept the theory that 'life owes you an automobile' is only to court disappointment, because a good many people will never get an automobile. To accept the doctrine that we are entitled to 'a good time' is to invite disillusionment, because few of us will find that life works out like that. Instead, sooner or later, almost all of us find that life is much more like a testing and perilous mountain climb than like a peaceful and hilarious picnic down in the sheltered valley.

I remember hearing a young officer describe the arrival of the first contingent of the relieving force at Belsen Concentration Camp. As they entered the gates and moved round the camp and saw the emaciated bodies and hopeless faces of the inmates, the appalling conditions of sordidness and starvation in which they were living, and the piles of unburied bodies of the dead, he said even he and his comrades, soldiers accustomed to harsh scenes, felt that the sight was almost more than they could bear.

But when Jesus used those words he was thinking of something more than the tribulation that belongs to our human lot, or the tribulation inseparable from awareness of the sufferings of our fellow-men. He was also warning his followers that in a special sense, and to a special degree, tribulation is inseparable from the highest kind of life.

The men to whom he spoke were all to find that true in their own experience. When they began truly to witness to Christ and proclaim his Kingdom, they had at once to face anger, scoffing, hatred, danger to life and limb, persecution, sometimes death.

I doubt if it is possible in any country, in any century, to live the Christian life of love to our neighbours, and obedience to God and his commandments, without tribulation.

One need not think only of imprisoned priests behind the Iron Curtain; but of young men and women in our own country who have accepted the Christian ideal of chastity in an age when loose sexual relationships no longer carry any stigma; of business men who, having accepted the Christian doctrine of the stewardship of money, deliberately reject opportunities of gain by questionable methods; of men engaged in industry who, having accepted the Christian doctrine of work, are determined to do their best and give of their best and have nothing to do with restrictive practices and 'working to rule'; of husbands and wives who, having taken Christian vows of marriage, refuse to find escape from domestic difficulties in a Divorce Court but would rather wrestle on through the tensions and trials in faith. Still, for those who in the modern world are seriously attempting to follow Christ and live the kind of life he taught, it is only too easy to understand what he meant when he said: "In the world you will have trouble."

"If the world hates you, it hated me first . . . As they persecuted me, they will persecute you."

What then does he mean by saying almost in the same breath, and to the same group of men:

"I have spoken thus to you, so that my joy may be in you, and your joy complete."?

Obviously this thing "Joy" of which he speaks is not pleasure, not fun and games, or a 'good time', as we often use these phrases. I think the secret of the joy which Jesus himself possesses is to be found in two things: his constant sense of the companionship of God and his sense of working in line with the purposes of God. In his whole ministry of teaching and compassion, with all its trials and tensions, its difficulties and disappointments, its taxing of both his physical strength and his faith, he is sustained and gladdened by the knowledge that through him the love of God is being enabled to reach out and help those in need. In that creative mission of compassion, he is continually conscious of God's Presence, and he finds joy: joy which he says that his followers can find also.

Do they find it? Well, when I try to think of the happiest people I know, they are rather a strange mixed company. I picture the mother of a large family, occupied from morning to evening with the endless tasks of running her house and looking after her husband and children. I picture a busy doctor, with hardly a moment of leisure from the time he gets up till nightfall, going from house to house where there is illness and pain. I picture an overworked and underpaid clergyman, whose parish covers a huge population of men and women and children, congested in countless sordid closes and narrow noisy streets, few of them at all religious but all of them desperately needing spiritual comfort and Christian care. I picture a schoolmaster, a bachelor with a class of tough East End boys of fourteen under his charge. Strangest of all, I think of an invalid woman, frail and helpless, never able to move from bed, yet always smiling, always interested in things far beyond her sick room, and always holding up others, the active healthy folk, in her love and prayers.

All these people have what I think Jesus meant by "Joy". They are happy people. In their lives, joy and tribulation are strangely mingled; in fact, sometimes so inextricably mingled that it is almost impossible to tell where one ends and the other begins!

It would seem, judging by such lives, that joy or true happiness depends not so much on having a good time or on material possessions, but in knowing that one is living a life of creative and compassionate work in line with God's purposes of love, and that in the doing of that work one has his approval and his companionship.

Some of you taking part in this act of worship are preparing and equipping yourselves for your life-work in many different spheres: teaching, medicine, law, scientific research, engineering. Each one of us will almost certainly be faced, whatever our calling, by testings and trials. Especially if we are resolved to follow Christ and accept the standards he has set and live in the spirit he showed, we shall know times of tribulation.

But also, without a shadow of doubt, we shall find joy; the joy of creative compassionate work, which we shall know to be in line with God's purposes of love, and work in which we shall know that day by day we can count upon his approval and his companionship.

THE PLACE OF AMBITION
IN THE CHRISTIAN LIFE

"The mother of Zebedee's sons then came before him, with
her sons. She bowed low and begged a favour. 'What is it
you wish?' asked Jesus. 'I want you', she said, 'to give orders
that in your kingdom my two sons here may sit next to you,
one at your right, and the other at your left'.

"When the others heard this, they were indignant with
the two brothers. So Jesus called them to him and said,
'You know that in the world, rulers lord it over their subjects, and their great men make them feel the weight of
authority; but it shall not be so with you. Among you,
whoever wants to be great must be your servant, and
whoever would be first must be willing slave of all—
like the Son of Man; he did not come to be served, but to
serve."

St. Matthew 20: 21, 24-28

Ambition is a common weakness. More than once, it is recorded
in the Gospels that the disciples of Jesus quarrelled as to who
among them should be the greatest. In this particular instance
it was the mother of two of them, James and John, who came
directly to Christ, asking that the two chief places in his Kingdom might be given to her two sons. It was a flagrantly selfish
ambition, and quite naturally evoked indignation among the
other members of the group. And from Jesus himself it elicited
not only a rebuke but one of the greatest of his sayings. The
standards and the prizes of the world, he says, are not his
standards and prizes. He holds before them a different ideal;
"Whoever would be first must be willing slave of all."

The saying leads us to ask: "What then is the place of
ambition in the life of a Christian man or woman, or is it to
have no place?" It is obvious that certain forms of ambition
are entirely unworthy. The mere desire for reputation and
honour for our own gratification, such as these two disciples
desired, is clearly unchristian. To some natures, this longing for
worldly success and prestige is a stronger temptation than to

others. "Fame is the spur." Such people will sometimes even sacrifice honour and truth in order to climb to the dazzling height upon which they have set their heart. So blinded are they by ambition, that they fail to realise how meretricious is honour thus attained. Even more unworthy is the insidious sordid ambition for wealth, which Paul stigmatises as a "root of all evil," and yet a root which can so easily entwine itself round our souls.

So again, the mere ambition to excel one's neighbours is wrong. Some modern educationists even condemn the awarding of prizes in school and university because, they say, the system of prizes begets an unhealthy system of rivalry; it forms in the mind of the young man or boy the thought that all life consists of competition. In the soul of the clever and successful it awakens conceit, and in the soul of the unsuccessful it begets discouragement and a sense of inferiority. Certainly this desire to surpass others is very deeply implanted in most of us. Yet it clearly conflicts with that ideal of humility and love that Jesus has shown us once for all to be the mark of the finest character.

Many of the evils and injustices of society in the past are due to this element of self-centred competition; to that form of ambition which involves a ruthless pushing aside of rivals, a trampling heedlessly upon the weak, an aggressive and selfish struggle to climb highest upon the ladder of success. How diametrically different is the ideal proclaimed by Jesus!

Jesus asked the disciples: "What were you arguing about on the way?" They were silent, because on the way they had been discussing who was the greatest. He sat down, called the Twelve, and said to them, "If anyone wants to be first, he must make himself last of all and servant of all." Then he took a child, set him in front of them, and put his arm round him. "Whoever receives one of these children in my name," he said, "receives me. For the least among you all—he is the greatest."

And yet we instinctively feel that there is a place for ambition even in the finest type of life. A man altogether without ambition seldom makes much contribution to the world. Is there then a right kind of ambition?

Ambition surely is right when it is a desire to use to their maximum our powers and endowments. This comes out in the lives of those who have had to develop their gifts in the face of adverse circumstances. For example, in the autobiography of H. G. Wells, he tells how at the age of twelve his father and mother could no longer afford to keep him at school and resolved to make him a draper's assistant. But from the beginning his soul revolted against this career. He had no interest in the price of calico or cotton. He had an insatiable thirst for knowledge. His mind was full of original fancies; his imagination was continually soaring away from his commonplace surroundings. Conscious of mental powers, he knew that, if he stayed in a draper's shop, these powers would be inevitably wasted. And the story of his early years of manhood is a constant struggle to escape out of the narrow sphere in which his parents had placed him into a sphere in which he would be able to use his gifts of mind and imagination. In the end his struggle was successful. At first in schoolmastering and later in journalistic and literary work, he was able to develop his endowments to their maximum, and give interest and pleasure to the thousands who read his books.

Similar is the case of Sir Henry Jones. His father was a village shoemaker in Wales, and when young Henry left school at the age of twelve, he "put on his little shoemaker's leather apron". But larger thoughts and dreams started in his brain. "I would become something better than a shoemaker, or I would die in the attempt."

He and his greatest friend, Tom Redfern, were walking together and talking late in the night.

"It was a lovely summer evening and all the world was asleep. When we were about a mile and a half from our village, on the bank of a little stream opposite some cottages, Tom and I shook hands over a solemn oath that some day we would be graduates of a University . . . It was a rather unusual proceeding for two boys of sixteen. And we kept our oath. A year or two after, I graduated in the Universty of Glasgow. Tom graduated at Cambridge."

And some years later still that shoemaker's son went to Glasgow University to occupy the Chair of Moral Philosophy, and became an honoured and beloved teacher, influencing generation by generation thousands of Scottish students for good. That story has been repeated again and again in the lives of those who have had to make their own way in the world against difficulties and hindrances, and whose dynamic perse_ verance has carried them to positions of influence and public service.

As Canon Pym has truly said:

"Our desire to get on in life is perfectly legitimate; and, up to a point, it is entirely beneficial to the community of which we are members, because it impels us to be producers and not merely consumers or parasites. The strength of the self-instinct in our nature is the primary incentive to work, to maintain our place in the swift current of life."

It is God who has given us our powers and gifts such as they are, and it is right that we should use them to the uttermost of our ability. The buried talent, the uncultivated gift, is wasted, whereas it was intended to be used for the glory of God and in the service of our neighbour. None of us has a right to be less than the best that it is in us to be. If there is peril in ambition, there is perhaps a greater peril in sloth. We all know men and women who should have made much more of their gifts and endowments than they have; who might have made a much higher and a much finer contribution to the world, if they had worked a little harder, if only they had not sat back so easily contented, but had been carried forward on the brave tide of enthusiasm.

What matters most of all in measuring the rightness or the wrongness of our ambitions is motive. Jesus was always more interested in motives than in actions. If in our ambitions we are actuated by solely selfish ends, whether that end be the longing for honour or reputation or power or wealth or high position, then our ambitions are unworthy; and, judged by the standards of Christ, must meet with his rebuke. William Temple once said: "To choose your career for selfish reasons is a worse sin than committing adultery for it is the withdrawal of the greater part of your time and energy from the service of God."

And as we look out into life and its prospects, there could, perhaps, be no more healthy act of self-examination than that we should ask ourselves sincerely from time to time: Is my ambition being directed towards the worthiest ends? Am I planning to use my talents for myself, or for God and my fellow-men? The consecrated ambition of a strong and gifted man or woman who has dedicated all his or her powers to some high purpose is a mighty force, and has been the dynamic and inspiration of most of the great reforming movements of history.

Have we not here then reached the Christian conception about the true use of our powers? Consecrated ambition, the desire to cultivate and use our talents to the very utmost, not in order to win personal honour, not to earn the applause of the world, not certainly to make money; but in order with those talents to serve our neighbours and glorify God. That is the only kind of ambition that Christ sanctions: "If anyone wants to be first, he must make himself last of all and servant of all." In every profession today, whether teaching or medicine, banking or business, there is urgent need for men and women whose chief motive is service to others.

Such ambition lifts a life to the highest levels. It is this high motive that marks off the really great statesman, for example, from those politicians who only seek high office for the personal prestige it will bring them. Selfish ambition has been and is one of the curses of public life. But if the standard of greatness suggested by Jesus our Lord were to prevail, how different things would be. According to his teaching the only man who is fit for high office is the man whose supreme desire is service to his fellows. We see this idea in great statesmen like Gladstone or Smuts, who stood out from their contemporaries, not so much by the supremacy of intellect, or the genius of administration, as by the sheer weight of their moral character, the common knowledge that they cared infinitely more for the good of the country and the high ideals they served than for their own career and reputation.

This principle holds throughout the whole range of public life. The desire for influence and leadership is only justified when a man is resolved to use his influence for worthy ends, for the service of the community, the removal or remedying of crying abuses, the raising of the standard of social life. Jesus, as always, has spoken the final word when he reminds us that the only true qualification for high position is readiness to serve.

THE PROBLEM OF PAIN

It may perhaps be asked, at the very beginning, whether the title of this paper is justified; is there in fact a problem of pain? I believe there is. Indeed it is a problem which has perplexed thoughtful minds almost since the beginnings of history. Moreover, like the mystery of death, it is a universal problem; not only of academic interest, moreover, but of urgent, practical importance. Because sooner or later, in larger or lesser degree, every man is confronted with pain. And if he is to have any adequate capacity to deal with life, then he must come to terms with this harsh fact, both in his thinking and in his behaviour. It is certainly also a very real and vital problem for anyone engaged in the pastoral ministry.

Let us look first briefly at pain simply as a given fact, a feature of this world as we know it. It is difficult to be certain about its range; to know for example whether it is possible to talk of plants or trees or even the lower forms of living creatures as being affected by pain. The humane angler will argue that the salmon he has caught does not really suffer, but at the same time he will see that it is given a death-blow as soon as possible after being landed on the river-bank!

When one comes to the higher animals, it is certain that they suffer pain; they show that they are capable of suffering and of fear (which is a genuine form of pain) and in our own country the Law makes cruelty to animals a punishable offence —although a great many people still seem strangely indifferent to the sufferings of animals, and some of us feel that laws and penalties for cruelty ought to be much more severe. The suffering of animals seems to me to constitute one of the most perplexing aspects of the problem of pain, although in this paper there will be no time to deal with it.

What is an indubitable fact is that the higher the rank in the scale of living creatures, and the more complex the organism, the greater is the capacity for pain. It is therefore natural that in Man, both as possessing the most complex physical and mental

M

constitution, and as the most highly self-conscious of all living creatures, one sees this fact of pain in its most acute form.

There are different types of pain, due to very varied causes: the pain caused by accident, the pain caused by cruelty, the pain caused by illness or old age, the pain caused by 'an act of God' such as an earthquake or a tornado or a stroke of lightning.

The suffering caused by accident constitutes no problem, for example the collision of two cars travelling at speed on the open road or a child left by itself and going too near to the fire, or the injury caused to a workman by the collapse of a badly-built wall. Such things are plainly due to human carelessness or inefficiency or fallibility of judgment.

The suffering caused by cruelty, on the other hand, creates at once an ultimate problem. Why does God allow his world to be spoilt in this way? Why did he not create a universe in which evil deeds were impossible, in which men and women always willed what was good and in accordance with his purposes of love?

Here of course we are confronted by the ultimate mystery, the insoluble problem of the existence of evil. Tentative answers can be suggested, although perhaps none of them is wholly satisfactory.

It can be argued, for example, that God is not really omni-potent; that there are evil forces in the universe which frustrate his will and again and again defeat his plans. That is the ancient theory of Manichaeism, which the Church early in its history rejected and branded as a heresy; and which Christian opinion still today in all parts of the world rejects.

Another explanation of evil, and one which seems to have the support of Holy Scripture, is that the possession of human free-will involves the possibility of wrong choices and wrong deeds.

In the book of Genesis we have a myth which attempts to give an explanation of the origin of evil. The world as God made it was good. All living creatures fulfilled their distinc-tive lives in harmony and happiness. Man, too, was created for happiness, but his happiness was dependent upon his willing obedience to God's laws. In the fair garden where dwelt the first man and woman there was a tree, the tree of the know-ledge of good and evil. The fruit of that tree was forbidden fruit. But the serpent pointed out to the Woman and the Man the beauty and attraction of that magic forbidden apple, weakened their resistance by specious arguments, and persuaded them to yield to temptation and disobey God's commandment. And as the first members of the human race used their gift of free-will to choose evil, so every member of the human race through the ages has followed their example. Nemesis followed. The perfection of God's creation was destroyed. Human life, instead of realising the Divine intention of peace and happiness, is marred by evil choices and actions and all the painful consequences which inevitably ensue.

When we turn to the pages of the New Testament and enquire what its writers have to say about suffering, and the pain that is the result of evil aims and actions, we see that they apparently accept this doctrine of the fall of Man and of original sin.

They assume that suffering is part of the lot of man in this present dispensation. They also seem to assume that the pain in the world is somehow connected with the evil in the world. One finds in the New Testament no metaphysical speculation as to whether God could have created a universe from which pain was altogether absent, whether this is in fact 'the best of all possible worlds'. They are realists and they are also men of faith. They accept the reality and inevitability of suffering in this earthly existence as we know it now. Its reality and inevitability are underlined in the life and death of Christ. Not even he, the Perfect Man, could evade it; he was in all points tested like as we are, although sinless. In his own body he felt the uttermost extremes of physical agony, right up to the point of death, identifying himself in this as in all things with our human lot.

Moreover, the New Testament writers all alike make it clear that Christ's acceptance of suffering was part of the unavoidable cost of the redemption of mankind. "He bore our sins in his own body, on the Tree." "By his stripes we are healed." What Adam, the first sinful man, had done he, the second Adam, the sinless Man, must undo:

> O loving wisdom of our God!
> When all was sin and shame,
> A second Adam to the fight,
> And to the rescue came.

> O Wisest love! that flesh and blood,
> Which did in Adam fail,
> Should strive afresh against the foe,
> Should strive and should prevail.

The Cross seems both to show how deeply pain is interwoven in the warp and woof of our human existence, and how inextricably sin and suffering are associated. Jesus also warns his followers that they too are to expect suffering and to be ready for it: "If the world hates you, it hated me first . . . As they persecuted me, they will persecute you." "In the world you will have trouble." Nor does he lead us to expect that things will get better. There is in fact nowhere in the New Testament (so far as I can see) any grounds for believing in the moral and spiritual progress of humanity, leading to easier and happy conditions of life. If we accept the apocalyptic sayings as authentic sayings of Christ, then clearly the opposite is true. Wickedness and suffering are likely to increase. "The whole created universe," says St. Paul, "groans in all its parts as if in the pangs of childbirth."

So much for the suffering caused, whether directly or indirectly, by human sin.

But there is also suffering due to illness.

In this connection there arises the question: What is the Christian view of illness and disease? It is argued by some writers, and it is the belief of many who are engaged in the so-called ministry of Spiritual Healing, that all disease is contrary to the will of God; and they argue in support of this belief that Christ our Lord during his earthly ministry seems to have healed every case of illness that was brought to him. It certainly cannot be questioned that Jesus' ministry among the towns and villages of Galilee was a ministry of healing as well as of preaching, and that he showed the utmost compassion and concern for those in bodily distress or infirmity. But on the other side, it is worth remembering that he could cure only a very small number of the multitudes of sick folk in the land, and that when, for example, he came to the Pool of Bethesda and stood among that sad company of disabled men and women, we are only told of his healing one man.

Moreover, all the facts of ordinary experience appear to suggest that illness is part of our human lot. This does not of course mean that it is to be passively accepted. Far from it. All the resources of medical skill and knowledge must be employed to combat disease wherever possible. Yet there are innumerable cases of illness where no cure is effected, and where scientific skill is baffled. And even if medicine were to make such advances in knowledge that it could treat all forms of disease with hope of success in the early and middle years, there would still remain the infirmities and illnesses inseparable from old age and the approach of death.

We seem then to be driven to the conclusion that illness and pain are part of our human lot in this present dispensation, and if not sent by God, yet permitted by the will of God. In this situation the Christian attitude will be one of both resistance and acceptance; doing everything possible in co-operation with the doctors to overcome the illness but at the same time ready if need be to accept it in serenity of spirit, and in unwavering confidence in God's power to "make all things work together for good to them that love him".

But can we go further than this? Can we believe that pain has certain positive values, which seem at least to alleviate the poignancy of the problem and to throw gleams of light on the mystery of suffering? I believe we can see such values, both at the lower and at the higher levels of experience.

It is a mistake to imagine that, even on the purely physical level, pain is always an evil thing. On the contrary, it has valuable uses as a warning of danger. A small child who plays with a sharp knife, a boy who in an excess of high spirits is tempted to tease the parrot, even a boisterous bullock trying to push his way through an electric fence, find that pain is a useful warning of danger. The hurt child will thereafter treat a sharp knife with respect; the boy will find it easier to resist the temptation to tease the parrot; the young bull will acquiesce more contentedly in his allotted pasture place.

Or again, in the field of medicine, the doctor regards pain as frequently an invaluable help in the detection and diagnosis of disease which might otherwise never have been suspected.

But it is when we consider the moral and spiritual levels of life that we can even better see the value of pain.

There is a strange, indeed a startling phrase, in the Epistle to the Hebrews, where the writer speaks of Jesus himself as 'being made "perfect through sufferings".' As though even he in his earthly life could not have reached the supreme spiritual heights without some experience of the darker, harsher, sterner aspects. If that was true of him, is it not infinitely more true of us sinful men and women?

Not that suffering in itself necessarily or inevitably purifies or strengthens character. It can, and often does, make a man bitter, hard, cynical. But if accepted in faith and courage, it does ennoble and purify. I think of a young man, a butcher by trade. At the age of about thirty-five, it was discovered that he had been attacked by creeping paralysis. The slow but inexorable advance of the deadly disease was a test which was doubly hard for one in the full strength of manhood. But he bore that test triumphantly. As I visited him month by month, I was conscious that although "the outward man was perishing, the inward man was being renewed day by day"; that while his physical infirmity increased, his character was undergoing a remarkable transformation, and he was growing in moral insight and maturity. Never once did I hear him complain at the trial that had overtaken him. His fortitude and cheerfulness were an inspiration to all who looked after him. Above all, his Christian faith seemed to deepen and strengthen. One day, shortly before the end, when he could no longer even feed himself or turn over the pages of a book, as I was leaving the room, he said to me, "How good God is!" Was he not indeed "made perfect through suffering?"

In the countries of the Western world today, with their almost vulgar material prosperity, there is in many quarters a revival of the creed of Hedonism; an assumption that man has a right to happiness, and a right in every possible way to avoid suffering. Whereas there is in fact no justification whatsoever for such a belief. If enjoyment of happiness, comfort, freedom from pain, were the true destiny of men and women on this earth, the world as we know it is singularly ill-fashioned to achieve that end.

That is certainly not the view of life that any of the Bible writers suggest. According to the teaching of Christianity, goodness, not happiness, is the goal to be aimed at. And those who have that goal in view must be prepared for effort, struggle, discipline, suffering. "The gate that leads to life is small and the road is narrow, and those that find it are few." It is indeed through the discipline of life's harder experiences that we are made morally and spiritually fit. But if we accept such life-discipline, not sullenly or resentfully as from a cruel fate, but patiently and bravely as from a wise loving Providence, then it will shape our character to a finer pattern. This is the argument of the passage in the Epistle to the Hebrews 12: 9-11:

"Again, we paid due respect to the earthly fathers who disciplined us; should we not submit even more readily to our spiritual Father, and so attain life? They discipline us for this short life according to their lights; but he does so for our true welfare, so that we may share his holiness. Discipline, no doubt, is never pleasant; at the time it seems painful, but in the end it yields for those who have been trained by it the peaceful harvest of an honest life."

Even a good earthly parent will often inflict punishment for wrongdoing on his child, or wish it to be inflicted when deserved and required. The sensible father will be quite satisfied to know that his son has been beaten by the schoolmaster for a serious misdemeanour, provided he knows that the master is a fair and responsible person. A young man who had committed a terrible crime here in Glasgow was after some days identified and arrested by the police, and the newspapers reported that his father had actually expressed relief that the arrest had taken place. Presumably because he knew that punishment was needed, and that perhaps only punishment could lead to reformation of the boy's character and life. The love that can chastise is the deepest kind of love, for in punishing it hurts itself. And if so, it is surely not impossible to believe that God, the infinitely loving, feels constrained to permit the suffering of us his so wayward children, to correct and purify and reform and bring us back to himself.

If so, then the demand for a world without pain is not only cowardly, but superficial. William James, in a famous and fascinating essay, gives a picture of the nearest approximation he knew to the hedonist's dream:

"A few summers ago I spent a happy week at the famous Assembly Grounds on the borders of Chautauqua Lake. The moment one treads that sacred enclosure, one feels one's self in an atmosphere of success. Sobriety and industry, intelligence and goodness, orderliness and ideality, prosperity and cheer-fullness, pervade the air. It is a serious and studious picnic on a gigantic scale. Here you have a town of many thousands of inhabitants, beautifully laid out in the forest and drained, and equipped with means for satisfying all the necessary lower and most of the superfluous higher wants of man. You have a first-class college in full blast. You have magnificent music—a chorus of seven hundred voices, with possibly the most perfect open-air auditorium in the world. You have every sort of athletic exercise from sailing, rowing, swimming, bicycling, to the ball-field and the more artificial doings which the gymnasium affords. You have kindergartens and model secondary schools. You have general religious services and special club-houses for the several sects. You have perpetually running soda water fountains, and daily popular lectures by distinguished men. You have the best of company, and yet no effort. You have no zymotic diseases, no poverty, no drunkenness, no crime, no police. You have culture, you have kindness, you have cheapness, you have equality, you have the best fruits of what mankind has fought and bled and striven for under the name of civilisation for centuries. You have, in short, a foretaste of what human society might be, were it all in the light, with no suffering and no dark corners.

"I went in curiosity for a day. I stayed for a week, held spellbound by the charm and ease of everything, by the middle-class paradise, without a sin, without a victim, without a blot, without a tear.

"But in this unspeakable Chautauqua there was no potentiality of death in sight anywhere, and no point of the compass visible from which danger might possibly appear. The ideal was so completely victorious already that no sign of any previous battle remained, the place just resting on its oars. . . Sweat and effort, human nature strained to the uttermost and on the rack, yet getting through alive, and then turning its back on its success to pursue another more rare and arduous still—this is the sort of thing the presence of which inspires us, and the reality of which it seems to be the function of all the higher forms of literature and fine art to bring home to us and suggest. At Chautauqua there were no racks, even in the place's historical museum; and no sweat, except possibly the gentle moisture on the brow of some lecturer, or on the sides of some player in the ball-field.

"Such absence of human nature *in extremis* anywhere seemed, then, a sufficient explanation for Chautauqua's flatness and lack of zest."

But how different from that hedonist's paradise is the world as we know it! This is in fact a dangerous universe, a universe full of hazards and heartbreaks and challenges, full of uncertainties and insecurities, a universe in which effort and struggle are frequently called for, and in which fortitude and patience and faith are qualities required for success; a universe moreover in which the finest achievements of character only seem to be attainable through suffering. As Canon Raven once put it:

"Without suffering there would be no sympathy, without pain no discipline or compassion, without struggle no progress. We who have known suffering have learnt to see that without it love would be meaningless and life insipid. We count the cost, and are content."

Even that inveterate cynic, Anatole France, recognised this truth:

"Pain is the grand educator of men. Pain taught them the arts, and poetry and morals. Pain inspired them with heroism and with pity. Pain gave life a new value in allowing it to be offered as a sacrifice; and pain, this august and gracious thing, has brought something of the infinite into human love."

Mr. Herbert Butterfield argues that the same is true on the wider arena of history:

"There is something very moving at times in Negro Spirituals —something which makes one feel that human nature under pressure can reach a creative moment, and find a higher end of life (if only in the arts) than the mere continuance of material comfort had seemed to offer them. It is not Old Testament doctrine, so far as I know, but it would seem that one of the clearest and most concrete of the facts of history is the fact that men of spiritual resources may not only redeem catastrophe, but turn it into a grand creative moment. It is hard to rid oneself of the impression that in general the highest vision and the rarest creative achievements of the mind must come from great internal pressure, and are born of a high degree of distress. In other words, the world is not merely to be enjoyed but is an arena for moral striving. If the end of history lies in personalities, which represent the highest things we know in the mundane realm, then we must face the fact that the purpose of history is not something that lies a thousand years ahead of us—it is constantly here, always with us, for ever achieving itself—the end of human history is the manufacture and education of human souls. History is the business of making personalities, even so to speak by putting them through the mill; and, though it fails us if we expect it to hand us happiness on a spoon, its very vicissitudes bring personality itself to a finer texture."[1]

Is this true even of the pain that is caused by man's wickedness and cruelty? In some sense at least, I believe it is.

One of the central convictions of Christianity is that out of what is in itself evil, good can be created. The supreme instance is of course the Cross. The crucifixion of Jesus Christ, the sinless Man by cruel, jealous, arrogant, sinful men, is in itself utterly evil; the most dastardly deed ever perpetrated in history. But as we have seen, by his acceptance of crucifixion with all its physical torture and mental anguish, by his confrontation of it in a spirit of faith in God, forgiveness for his torturers, and compassion for the whole sinful race of mankind, Jesus brought out of it incalculable spiritual good. So that, lifted up from the earth upon that Cross, he has been able to draw countless souls to him, and reconcile them to God. And even by his example of fortitude and charity, how marvellously he has strengthened others in their time of trial and tribulation.

Surely it looks as though God, having decided to risk creating a world into which evil and pain might find entrance, chose not to destroy the work of his hands as something now utterly useless and disappointing, but instead to send his own Son to share the world's pain and turn it to good!

Similarly does Christianity teach that it is possible for us men and women to create out of even suffering caused by wickedness and cruelty, moral and spiritual good which perhaps could not otherwise have been achieved. One need only think of Sidney Carton (in *A Tale of Two Cities*) going to face the guillotine with that famous sentence on his lips: "It is a far, far better thing that I do than I have ever done. It is a far, far better place that I go to than I have ever known." One thinks of a woman like Edith Cavell who, through her trial by a rough military tribunal and her brave death at the hands of a firing squad, made a contribution not only to the traditions of the nursing profession, but to the ideal of compassionate service which could have been achieved at no less cost.

[1] *Christianity and History.* By kind permission of G. Bell & Sons Ltd.

Even in our own limited experience, within the circle of our acquaintances and friends, is it not in those who have known the sterner, harder experiences of life that we recognise a strength of character, a depth of spiritual insight, a charity of outlook which is often lacking in those born with a silver spoon in their mouth and apparently exempt from pain, disappointment, anxiety, sorrow?

If so, are we not driven (driven reluctantly, for it is an unpalatable doctrine) to the conviction that the Bible thinkers are right, that God has permitted pain in his universe as the Great Educator, a tutor whose discipline we could only dispense with at our moral peril. Here are some sentences from C. S. Lewis's fascinating, brilliant essay on this subject:

"My own experience is something like this. I am progressing along the path of life in my ordinary contentedly fallen and godless condition, absorbed in a merry meeting with my friends for the morrow or a bit of work that tickles my vanity today, a holiday or a new book, when suddenly a stab of abdominal pain that threatens serious disease, or a headline in the newspapers that threatens us all with destruction, sends this whole pack of cards tumbling down. At first I am overwhelmed, and all my little happinesses look like broken toys. Then slowly and reluctantly, bit by bit, I try to bring myself into the frame of mind that I should be in at all times. I remind myself that all these toys were never intended to possess my heart, that my true good is in another world and my only real treasure is Christ. And perhaps, by God's grace, I succeed, and for a day or two become a creature consciously dependent on God and drawing its strength from the right sources. But the moment the threat is withdrawn, my whole nature leaps back to the toys. I am even anxious, God forgive me, to banish from my mind the only thing that supported me under the threat because it is now associated with the misery of those few days. Thus the terrible necessity of tribulation is only too clear. God has had me for but forty-eight hours and then only by dint of taking everything else away from me. Let him but sheathe that sword for a moment and I behave like a puppy when the hated bath is over—I shake myself as dry as I can, and race off to reacquire my comfortable dirtiness, if not in the nearest manure heap, at least in the nearest flower bed. And that is why tribulations cannot cease until God either sees us remade or sees that our remaking is now hopeless."[1]

We reach here the deepest paradox of the Christian faith, in fact, the deepest paradox of life itself: that pain is both an evil and at the same time the path to salvation and purification. Jeremiah says: "It is good for me that I have been afflicted: that I might learn thy statutes." Here is the only realistic and the only satisfying answer (even though it be only a partial answer) to the age-long problem of pain, with which the thinkers have wrestled through the centuries. As Nicholas Berdyaev says:

"Buddhism and Stoicism are afraid of suffering and teach how to avoid it, how to become insensible to it, and dispassionate . . . Christianity has the courage to accept the pain and the suffering. Buddhism has not, and therefore it renounces existence and seeks refuge in non-being. Nietzsche says that it is not so much the suffering as the senselessness of it that is unendurable. Man can go through the most terrible sufferings, if he sees a meaning in them. Christianity gives meaning to suffering and makes it endurable . . . Suffering is bound up with sin and evil, just as death is. But it is also the way of redemption, of light and regeneration: to accept suffering is the cross which everyone must bear, following the Crucified. This is the deepest mystery of Christianity and of Christian ethics."[2]

But no consideration of the problem of pain from the Christian angle is complete if our gaze is limited by the horizons of this earthly scene. Because Christianity has a longer perspective. And again and again the different writers of the New Testament documents remind us of this. "For I reckon," says St. Paul, "that the sufferings we now endure bear no comparison with the splendour, as yet unrevealed." "Now we see only puzzling reflections in a mirror, but then we shall see face to face. My knowledge now is partial; then it will be whole, like God's knowledge of me."

Some people profess to see a morally dangerous and unsatisfactory element in this Christian attitude; as though it involved acquiescence in all sorts of injustices in this world, on the understanding that in the next world there would be compensations.

---

[1] *The Problem of Pain.* By kind permission of Geoffrey Bles Ltd.
[2] *The Destiny of Man.* By kind permission of Geoffrey Bles Ltd.

But the writers of the New Testament, as we have seen, suggest nothing of the sort. Rather they seem steadfastly to stand by two fundamental convictions:

First. That this present earthly life is a kind of spiritual apprenticeship for the further stages of life beyond, and that in this apprenticeship the discipline of pain and suffering seems to be a necessary element. In other words, Keats is essentially Christian in his assertion that this world is "a vale of soul-making".

The other certainty to which they hold is that our perspective is completely distorted if we look at human life as confined within the limits of three score years and ten. The whole Christian doctrine of Man gives the lie to any such assumption. We men are made in the image of God, made capable of fellowship with God, made for eternal life in communion with God—if we desire it. "What is man's chief end? Man's Chief End is to glorify God and enjoy him forever."

These wider horizons constitute the key to the Christian view of evil and suffering as we see them on the larger scale of world history, no less than as we see and experience them in our own individual lives. In this brief essay, it has only been possible to think of the problem of pain as it affects individual men and women. But to many people the problem seems even more acute when seen on the vast panorama of human history. The carnage of the battlefield, the cruelty of concentration camps, the misery of millions of refugees and displaced persons, the desolation caused by some deadly epidemic, the hunger of backward, over-populated countries—how is it possible to reconcile such harsh facts with the belief that there is a just and merciful Governor of the universe?

The Christian philosophy declares that you cannot find the final answer to that problem within history itself, but only beyond history. It is impossible to understand the Christian outlook if one ignores this eschatological perspective. The Christian Church has always held to the doctrine of the Second Coming of Christ, even although at times it may have been unpopular or may have seemed absurd to advocates of a liberal or scientific theology. Thus even B. H. Streeter writes:

"It seems certain that our Lord anticipated the complete

destruction of the existing world order, involving the dis-
appearance both of the Roman Empire and of the religious
system which had its centre in the Temple of Jerusalem—the
highest embodiments of the then existing civilisation on its
political and its religious sides respectively. This was to be
followed by a New Era of blessedness in a reconstituted and
spiritually renovated world, the initiation of which is associated
with his own return."

Whether that return is to be conceived of as happening 'in
instalments' beginning with the Day of Pentecost or in some
single great Divine action, constituting a virtual winding-up
of the process of history as we know it, its significance remains
the same: it will mean the final triumph of Christ over all the
forces of evil and suffering. The Cross and resurrection have
already, within the process of history, given a foretaste and
promise of that ultimate Divine victory: and have provided the
assurance of its completion. J. S. Whale well sums it up:

"The emphasis of Christian eschatology is twofold. On the
one hand it proclaims that the End has already been realised.
The Word became flesh and dwelt among us and we behold
His Glory. The New Testament rings with the proclamation
that the final outcome of history has already happened. The
Age To Come is here, with power and great glory. If any man
is in Christ, there the new creation, the Age To Come, is. He
has tasted of its powers. Christ has rescued us out of the
Dominion of Darkness and transferred us into the Kingdom of
the Son of his Love. The Kingdom of God has come upon us.

"Nevertheless the New Testament also looks to a future
consummation, the final judgment, an End which is not yet, an
eternal order of blessedness in God of which our Christian life
in time is the foretaste and the first fruits.

"The New Testament speaks, therefore, not only of Christ's
coming in Bethlehem, nineteen centuries ago, but also of his
second coming. Christian doctrine teaches a *geminus adventus*, a
twofold event, reminding men that the Christian life is lived
in terms of this tension, between what has happened and what
will happen: between this world where we have surely seen
the light of the knowledge of God's glory in the face of Christ
and the world to come where the whole meaning of Christian

history as the accomplishment of God's purpose will be revealed in the Last Judgment.

"Bunyan's characteristic word, 'the milk and honey is beyond this wilderness' is what all great Christians have said."[1]

Towards this divine consummation all the New Testament writers point, with variety of language but with astonishing unanimity of conviction and faith.

"I charge you to obey your orders irreproachably and without fault until our Lord Jesus Christ appears. That appearance God will bring to pass in his own good time—God who in eternal felicity alone holds sway. He is King of kings and Lord of lords" (I Tim. 6: 14-15).

"So Christ was offered once to bear the burden of men's sins, and will appear a second time, sin done away, to bring salvation to those who are watching for him" (Hebrews 9: 28).

"Be patient, my brother, until the Lord comes. The farmer looking for the precious crop his land may yield can only wait in patience, until the winter and spring rains have fallen. You too must be patient and stout-hearted, for the coming of the Lord is near" (James 5: 7-8).

"Since the whole universe is to break up in this way, think what sort of people you ought to be, what devout and dedicated lives you should live! Look eagerly for the coming of the Day of God and work to hasten it on; that day will set the heavens ablaze until they fall apart, and will melt the elements in flames. But we have his promise, and look forward to the new heavens and a new earth, the home of justice" (II Peter 3: 11-13).

"Then I saw a new heaven and a new earth, for the first heaven and the first earth had vanished, and there was no longer any sea. I saw the holy city, New Jerusalem, coming down out of heaven from God, made ready like a bride adorned for her husband. I heard a loud voice proclaiming from the throne: 'Now at last God has his dwelling among men! He will dwell among them and they shall be his people, and God himself will be with them. He will wipe every tear from their

---

[1] *Christian Doctrine.* By kind permission of the Cambridge University Press.

eyes; there shall be an end to death, and to mourning and crying and pain; for the old order has passed away' " (Revelation 21: 1-4).

Here, in its cosmic aspect, is the final Christian answer to the problem of suffering.